The Absolute Inheritance Ta......ng

Steve Parnham

Disclaimer

Please note that this book is intended as general guidance only for individual readers and does not and cannot constitute accountancy, tax, legal, investment or any other professional advice. The author accepts no responsibility or liability for loss which may arise from any person acting or refraining from action as a result of anything contained in this book.

The tax legislation and practice of HM Revenue & Customs is constantly changing and evolving. You are recommended to contact a suitably qualified tax adviser, solicitor, accountant, independent financial adviser or other professional adviser for tax, legal, accountancy, financial or other advice. Such an adviser will issue you with a letter of engagement specifically tailored to your needs and request the necessary information and details of your circumstances from you. You should also be aware that your personal circumstances will invariably vary from the general examples given in this book and that your professional adviser will be able to give specific advice based on your personal circumstances.

This book covers UK taxation and any references to 'tax' or 'taxation' in this book, unless the contrary is expressly stated, are to UK taxation only.

CONTENTS

"Sacred cows make the best hamburger "

Abbie Hoffman 1936-1989

Preface

The former Labour MP Roy Jenkins once quipped in 1986 that, "Inheritance tax is a voluntary levy paid by those who distrust their heirs more than they dislike the Inland Revenue".

It is a great line but in my experience it is wide of the mark when it comes to reality. Who would do that? It is, nevertheless, spot on when it comes to the perception of the family members left behind.

It would be more accurate to say that, "Inheritance tax is a voluntary levy effectively paid for by the families and loved ones of the deceased as a consequence the deceased's proclivity for doing only what they are inclined to do in the short term." That proclivity is crucially that of the person who has died, of course, but it could often equally be said to extend to other family members themselves. Change the mindset, even slightly, and the outcome will be different, very different.

The most obvious aspect of an ineffective mindset for inheritance tax planning is a propensity to focus solely on the short term, on things that are coming over the horizon today and that are clearly visible, rather on those things which are way beyond the horizon. The problem with planning for tax in general is that most people tend to focus on it when the effects are imminent. It may be a transaction which has just occurred or will shortly occur, for instance. Most people also tend to think of tax in terms of annual cycles whether that is the preparation of accounts or tax returns and it is not particularly intuitive to think strategically in much longer periods of time.

Inheritance tax is not an everyday tax and can be justifiably thought of as both ambiguous and complex. What has become known as private client work in professional circles has a deserved reputation for being one of the most intellectually challenging areas of tax advice.

With inheritance tax we are looking at an event sometime in the future and at a liability which the person with the exposed assets will not personally suffer or even witness during their lifetimes. That makes it a more difficult prospect to deal with, it appears less tangible, and for many it borders on the impossible as a consequence.

For all these reasons, it is inevitable that inheritance tax tends to occupy a place at the back of many people's minds, including professional minds. However, the cost is very real and steps can be taken to address the impact for your family and close friends, assuming of course you like them more than the Inland Revenue as HM Revenue & Customs were known when Roy Jenkins was writing.

Part I. The Four Horsemen of the Apocalypse

"For every complex problem there is an answer that is clear, simple, and wrong."

H. L. Mencken 1880-1956

If you intend to stand impotently on the side-lines with regard to inheritance tax planning then you should be aware of the extremely proactive (and extreme) characters who will appear on the scene shortly before your demise.

The next five chapters give a flavour of what you and your family may see approaching in your final moments.

Chapter 1. Dying Without Planning for Inheritance Tax

In the real world the blunt and brutal fact is that a stopwatch starts ticking on the day after you die. It stops just over six months later. That is the day your family must pay the inheritance tax due on your estate.

These circumstances will doubtless appear as manifestly unfair to your family but the tax burden is simply a fact of life and of death. It is predictable. It has been so in various guises for at least many hundreds of years. Death has always been a convenient time for the authorities to tax a person. It is also their very last chance to do so. They will make it count! If you do nothing to address that completely predictable and quantifiable liability the reality is this is what you will be remembered for by your heirs. Doing nothing. The family will feel that they will earn their, considerably impaired, legacy by sorting out the mess you have left behind.

If your family needs to obtain probate, and they will where your assets include shares or property regardless of the value of your estate, tax may well be due at the time of the probate application itself. That is likely to be little more than a few weeks after you die. The crucial issue for the family is therefore how on earth to pay the tax.

If you are single and own assets worth more than £325,000, any investment property or a business then there will be tax to pay. If you and your spouse or civil partner own more than £650,000 there will be tax to pay. From April 2017 if you own a home then, under the right circumstances, there is a further allowance available to set against that asset. Anything above these thresholds will be taxed at 40%. Do a simple calculation right now. Make a list of your assets and their current values, deduct the nil rate band(s) available to you and take 40% of that. This is the sum at stake and it is the sum by which the estate you have left will be reduced. For practical purposes you may as well have left a legacy to HM Revenue & Customs. Really? Well, that is what your family will think!

The tax on property and certain shares can be paid by instalments over several years but most people feel that is a just a bit too much like taking out another mortgage in practice. Psychologically most will also seek closure following your demise and dragging things out may look profoundly unattractive. Generally, therefore, this tends not to happen. Where the value of your estate is concentrated in property or shares including those in your own company the result is often hasty sales or liquidations to obtain the necessary funds. There will be no succession to an intact family business in these circumstances. At a difficult emotional time for the family they are also faced with impossible decisions – it is not quite the legacy they or you might have anticipated.

It is not just that the estate passing to the family is significantly less, perhaps 25% or 30% less than everyone thought as a consequence of the tax. It is the very practical issue of having to sell the family jewels or take out loans to pay for the tax.

It can be a bit like witnessing a slow motion, concertina style train crash. Over the decades while you are ruminating on your estate, the movement of the train is so imperceptible that there is little sense of motion at all. That all changes on the day you die. For observers, the train now instantly accelerates towards a catastrophic impact within weeks or a few months at most. The momentum built up over those decades of inactivity suddenly becomes all too visible. The uncontrollable inevitability of the damage over such a short time span makes it very dramatic for those left behind to witness it.

Can you change that unintentional legacy? Can you protect your wealth, possibly built up over more than one generation, from tax at these levels?

There are two answers to this question.

One is simple. "Death is the solution to all problems. No man - no problem." - Joseph Stalin.

But would you take tax advice from this man? Do nothing and you might as well have done.

In almost every case the true and accurate answer is 'yes' so long as you are prepared to adopt an alternative and more engaged perspective from the one underlying the generic shrug and the view that, "It is not my problem." The decisive factor is invariably whether you have that perspective or whether you can learn it and acquire it.

Chapter 2. Dying Without a Will

If you do not have a will then you are in good company. There are many in the public domain who have failed to do this and you will have heard of most of them. Abraham Lincoln, Martin Luther King, Howard Hughes, Pablo Picasso, Bob Marley, Kurt Cobain, Barry White, Stieg Larsson, James Brown, Amy Winehouse, Jimi Hendrix and Rik Mayall to name but a handful.

Most of these celebrities probably just 'did not get around to it' but some also did not bother on principle. In practice one often finds that an absence of planning goes hand in hand with the absence of a will ... or a poorly drafted one.

One of the most recent public cases of someone dying without a will is that of Prince. It is thought that Prince never made a will because he was scared of being 'screwed over' by putting his signature on legal documents, and is said to have become 'paranoid' after having had problems with contracts in his younger years while he was still an emerging star.

"Record contracts are just like - I'm gonna say the word - slavery," he once said, according to Rolling Stone. "I would tell any young artist. Don't sign." It was a rebellion against Prince's record label, Warner Bros. He first signed with the company back in 1977 when he was still a teenager, and together they produced some of his most famous titles, including Purple Rain and Sign O the Times.

But after signing a new deal in the early 1990s, Prince found the company's production schedule very difficult. A prolific songwriter, he particularly wanted to release material as soon as it was ready - he had some 500 unreleased songs in his famous studio vault. However, Warner Bros refused to release them, believing it would saturate the market and dilute demand for the artist's music.

"He felt the contracts at the time were onerous and burdensome," said John Kellogg, assistant chair of the music business management department at Berkley College of Music. "He rebelled against that."

This scepticism spilled over into other aspects of his life and was probably a major influence in his decision not to prepare a will. It is a surprising decision since a will would have allowed him to call the shots … something one would have thought he would embrace to avoid his legacy being 'screwed over'.

In the US, absence of a will means that the estate goes into probate and falls under the jurisdiction of the state. In this case Bremer Bank was appointed as special administrator to determine the heirs. Under Minnesota law, the estate of a person with no spouse, children or parents would be split amongst siblings.

Whatever the reason, the point is the stark consequences of dying intestate. What happens to your estate is then decisively out of your hands. Intestacy law will determine who gets what, which may well be at variance with what you and your family would have wished, and the tax position will invariably not be the best that could have been achieved.

In the UK someone who dies without a will is subject to the rules of intestacy, but the law varies depending on where you live.

If you live in England and Wales and Northern Ireland, a surviving spouse generally receives a priority legacy of £250,000 together with all personal possessions and 50% of the remaining estate, as long as they are married or in a civil partnership. Surviving children receive the other half of the estate.

As a consequence it is not uncommon for bereaved spouses to be forced to bring legal proceedings or 'friendly litigation' against their own children to be able to stay in the family home. The intestacy rules do not allow the spouse to have everything automatically and the spouse may not end up with enough to stay in the home. It is difficult, unpleasant and costly to sue your own children.

A relative who wants to deal with the estate of someone who has died but left no will usually must apply for letters of administration from the probate registry. There are strict rules on who can be an administrator with priority starting with married spouses and civil partners, followed in descending order by children, grandchildren, parents, siblings, nephews & nieces and finally other relatives. Unmarried partners are excluded from the process.

In Scotland a surviving spouse also has first claim to the estate in the absence of a will, but there are limitations. A partner would only automatically inherit your interest in a single property at values up to £473,000 when you die. That means if you have two properties, your spouse would only inherit one of these.   The remainder would go to your children or otherwise may pass to siblings or parents.

In Scotland the principle of Legal Rights applies to every estate, meaning that every child and spouse has a claim, even if there is a will. If there is not, an executor would have to be appointed by the court. Unmarried partners have no automatic claim to an inheritance. The bereaved partner would have to apply to the court within six months of the death under the Family Law Scotland Act 2006 and the court would have complete discretion as to what to allow them, up to the maximum that a spouse would automatically be entitled to.

A dependant of the deceased can apply to the court under the Inheritance (Provision for Family and Dependants) Act 1975.

Co-habitees are only able to claim what is necessary for their maintenance, whereas married spouses would not be limited to this.

It is thought that about 60% - 70% of people in the UK do not have a will. According to a recent YouGov survey, nearly two thirds of the British adult population are in this position. According to the YouGov survey of 1,794 adults, 38% of the public in England and Wales had a will in 2015, up from 35% in 2014.

The number of enquiries concerning people who people who have died without making a will has more than doubled over the past five years, according to Citizens Advice. Citizens Advice told BBC 5 Live Daily in May 2016 that it had 1,522 such queries in 2011 but 3,747 in 2015.

The Tax Implications of Intestacy

Leaving no will invariably leaves a real mess for those left behind but it also has serious tax implications. Let us look at an example of what can happen in practice.

Let's assume that James left an estate that was worth around £1.2 million. As he had not left a will, the whole of his estate does not automatically pass to his widow as both partners would have liked. Instead it is divided between his widow and three children according to the rules of intestacy.

His widow inherits the first £250,000, with no inheritance tax to pay, because inheritance tax is not payable on legacies between spouses.

When James dies is quite important. If he died before October 2014, James's widow would inherit a "life interest", effectively a trust interest, in £250,000, and one half of the rest of his estate, again with no inheritance tax to pay. Had James passed away after October 2014, his widow would have inherited that sum absolutely, not just for life, as a result of the change in the intestacy rules in October 2014.

She also inherits 50% of the excess, that is £475,000.

His children inherit the remaining £475,000 between them – but this is where it all starts to go wrong in practical and in tax terms.

Although legacies between spouses are tax free, inheritance tax is payable on legacies to children. The first £325,000 passes to his children tax free as a result of his nil rate band (see Chapter 10), but the tax is 40% of anything over and above that amount. i.e. £425,000 - £325,000 at 40%. Not only has James's widow lost a significant part of her husband's estate to other family members, not at all what most people intend to happen, but through his inaction James has effectively left what amounts to a legacy of £60,000 to the Treasury. That is 5% of his estate.

So, the net effect of £475,000 of James's estate passing to his children is that inheritance tax becomes payable on the excess of £150,000 - a £60,000 tax bill! That £60,000 could instead have been used to contribute towards his widow's financial security if only James had written the right kind of will.

Whether everything passes to James's widow or not does not affect the overall amount of tax due on the second death of the couple, of course, assuming that for these purposes the values remain the same. What it does do in a very visible sense is to accelerate the payment of tax on that element which does not go to the survivor in excess of the nil rate band .... in other words the couple pay inheritance tax some time and perhaps a couple of decades earlier than is necessary.

So there are actually two issues here. Not only does the deceased's partner only get a part of the estate; there is also often an accelerated and unnecessary tax payment to deal with.

The Immediate Fix

Is there a way out of this trap for James's widow?

Yes there is, potentially. Provided all three of the children agree (which they may not), and provided action is taken before the second anniversary of James's death. A deed of variation can be drawn up, passing the whole of the James's estate to his widow. That would give her the security of the full £1.2 million to live on, delaying any inheritance tax liability until the end of her life.

On her death, James's widow's £325,000 nil rate band is added to James's unused nil rate band, so that the children could inherit the first £650,000 before paying inheritance tax.

As for the excess over and above that £650,000, yes, inheritance tax would be payable at 40%. If the estate were still worth £1.2 million on her death, the inheritance tax bill would be £220,000.

What has happened though as a result of dying intestate is that £60,000 of that tax has been paid today, or rather within six months of James's death, rather than on the death of his wife. That is a very big payment on account. The deed of variation rectifies the position.

If a deed of variation were executed along the suggested lines, James' widow would also have the option of considering a little planning during her lifetime to reduce that £220,000 tax. She could simply spend it during her lifetime and she could make substantial gifts to the children and, provided she lived on for a further seven years, those gifts would serve to reduce the inheritance tax.

She could also take out a life insurance policy in favour of the executors of her will, written in trust to prevent it being taxed itself, that pays out £220,000 to her executor, which they would then use to pay the tax bill. She would have to take advice and do her sums, as to whether the premiums were cost effective. The younger and fitter you are when you take out a policy like this, the lower the premiums.

In a nutshell, a well drafted will allows the estate to pass between spouses or civil partners tax free as you would probably intend and for the survivor to then take some action to mitigate the eventual tax bill.

Chapter 3. Dying With a Poorly Drafted Will

About 15% of people who do have a will have had no professional help in drawing it up. By implication, it will almost certainly never be reviewed for changing circumstances and legislation.

This DIY route may have saved a few hundred pounds in solicitors fees some years ago but it is often a false economy. Common mistakes in 'do it yourself' wills include wrongly identifying beneficiaries or assets, failing to appoint executors, failing to deal with all the estate, using incorrect legal terms, failing to update it for family and legislative changes and not having the will properly witnessed. Any of these basic errors would invalidate a will if it was legally challenged .... and then we are back to deeds of variation and intestacy.

A waste of effort.

The Issue of Disinheritance

If you do have a will it is usually sensible not to overtly side line dependent family members without good reason or, if you need to do this, to plan for it in your lifetime. Contesting a will is not only emotionally draining with all the risks of family tension, but it is also a costly and very time consuming process. Anyone considering omitting a spouse, civil partner or close family member from their will would be well advised to consider whether that could ultimately lead to a dispute and court proceedings.

What may have been a tight family unit beforehand can become divided, sometimes irreparably, as a result of a dispute. Attempting to cut a spouse or child out of a will, or leaving them little, may offer them no alternative but to bring a claim against other family members. You should never underestimate the sense of entitlement once you have departed.

If you do side line someone, then your will may be contested under the Inheritance (Provision for Family and Dependants) Act 1975 in circumstances where the deceased may be considered to have failed to provide reasonable financial provision for someone who is eligible to bring a claim. If successful, the other beneficiaries will receive less than they were originally bequeathed. These claims can sometimes be avoided with a well-written will and an ancillary 'statement of reasons' to support its content. This is particularly prudent where the testator is excluding estranged family members from the will. A statement of reasons that has been carefully drafted, and signed by the testator, will have gravitas and will be considered by a judge when deciding whether to award provision.

You might therefore consider who could be entitled to a claim, so that an informed discussion and statement can be prepared to prevent unwanted litigation as far as possible.

High Court disputes between family members over inheritance have reached a record high, according to recent figures.

The number of High Court cases brought under the Inheritance (Provision for Family and Dependents) Act 1975 reached 116 in 2015, an 11.5 per cent increase on 2014, when there were 104 High Court claims. The number of claims has increased by a factor of eight since 2005, when just 15 cases were heard in the High Court.

We are seeing a growing number of cases where people are seeking legal remedy as a result of being left out of a will entirely, or receiving less than they expected, either as a deliberate act on the part of the deceased or because a family member died without having made a will. Modern family structures are making inheritance claims increasingly likely. People are more likely to marry multiple times, or cohabit outside of marriage, and if there are children or stepchildren involved, the likelihood of someone feeling hard done by is even greater than before. Contentious probate is one of the fastest growing areas in the professional world. Regrettably, this type of litigation will undoubtedly delay the administration of an estate, possibly by some years, which will seem manifestly unfair to the original beneficiaries.

Until the intestacy laws are updated to reflect modern family life, more people will make claims on deceased estates.

In a recent case, a statement of reasons had been prepared but it was considered not determinative. With the benefit of hindsight it could be seen that the statement of reasons that had been prepared was based on negative reasons as to why the claimant should be excluded – it did not emphasise positive reasons as to why the other beneficiaries should have received their bounty. As an illustration, if the testatrix or testator had been a lifelong supporter of animal charities this reason could have carried more weight.

The case highlights the importance of providing a concise and objective statement when a potential claimant is being excluded from the will, in case it is challenged later.

The ruling also highlights the fact that even when adult children have been deliberately disinherited, it is still possible to challenge the will of the deceased. The ruling has been seen by some commentators as a source of encouragement to adult children who have been left out of a will or not provided for to any great extent, to seek to challenge their deceased parent's decision, whether that decision was set out in a written will or by deciding not to make a will at all and leaving the distribution of their estate to the laws of intestacy.

Although a well drafted statement cannot be determinative, a court will take it into account when deciding whether a potential claimant has a valid claim.

It is perhaps worth setting out the background to a high profile case and the decision of The Supreme Court in March 2017.

Ilott v The Blue Cross and Others, centred on Heather Ilott, who had been excluded from her mother Melita Jackson's will. Jackson left most of her estate, worth around £500,000, to three charities – The Blue Cross, the RSPCA and the RSPB. Jackson had excluded her daughter after she left home with a boyfriend as a 17-year-old.

Ilott challenged the will under the 1975 act and was awarded £50,000.

Both parties appealed: Ilott claimed she had not been awarded enough while the charities said there was no lack of reasonable provision in the judgement.

On appeal, Ilott, was awarded £143,000 - to buy the rented home she was living in - plus an extra £20,000 for additional income. The Court of Appeal said Ilott, who had five children and was on benefits and without a pension, was not given a reasonable provision in the will.

The Supreme Court found in March 2017 that the Court of Appeal erred when calculating reasonable financial provision and allowed the charities' appeal against that decision. The ruling, unanimous with a supplementary judgement from Lady Hale, restores the original order handed down by District Judge Clive Million.   Ilott would now receive the original £50,000 award.

In her supplementary judgement, Lady Hale observed: 'I have written this judgement only to demonstrate what, in my view, is the unsatisfactory state of the present law, giving as it does no guidance as to the factors to be taken into account in deciding whether an adult child is deserving or undeserving of reasonable maintenance. I regret that the Law Commission did not reconsider the fundamental principles underlying such claims when last they dealt with this topic in 2011.'

On the one hand, adult children of a deceased will continue to be able to seek redress from the courts where a will or the rules of intestacy fail to make reasonable financial provision for them. On the other hand, it was never intended that the legislation should act as a springboard for disgruntled adult children to challenge their parents' testamentary freedom, just because they consider a will's dispositions to be unfair. The Supreme Court justices have confirmed this is the case.

While the judgement undoubtedly represents a victory for testamentary freedom, it should equally be recognised that an adult child in her 50's succeeded in securing what amounted to 10% of her mother's estate even though she was excluded from the will. She came within a whisker of securing a third of the estate.

Citizens Advice told BBC 5 live Daily in May 2016 that it had experienced a rise in queries about problems executing wills from 8,160 about executing wills in 2011 rising to 11,137 in 2015.

Chapter 4. Losing Mental Capacity

The ability to make a will and make gifts to loved ones is something which most of us take for granted (even if we do not do anything about it). So is the opportunity during lifetime to plan for the ultimate inheritance tax liability. We have looked at some of the consequences of failing to plan for inheritance tax or failing to have a will ... or both.

The issue of a lack of planning and the absence of a will invariably produce their greatest impact when the individual dies but the effect can be even more excruciating should you lose mental capacity. If this happens responsibility for both wills and tax planning can pass to your attorney(s) and their capacity to take proper decisions on your behalf and for the family may well be highly restricted by what you have done or failed to do previously. You will then actually experience the effects of doing nothing in your lifetime.

Consider what the position would be if you lacked mental capacity without either having made a will or undertaken any planning for the inheritance tax liability before you lose capacity. Even the most basic planning is considerably restricted for Attorneys and Deputies acting on behalf of someone who lacks mental capacity. Extra care needs to be taken to make sure that they are not exceeding their authority. For wills and anything more than a modest gift, an application to the Court of Protection will be needed.

Do not underestimate just how much of a straightjacket your family will find themselves in.

Let us look at some of the specifics.

Making gifts

An attorney appointed by a Lasting Power of Attorney or a Deputy appointed by the Court of Protection will have wide powers to deal with the financial affairs of the person who lacks mental capacity. However, these powers are not unlimited and are particularly restricted when it comes to making gifts.

Inheritance tax planning by making gifts works by reducing the value of the estate so that less inheritance tax is payable. This can be effective provided that the donor survives seven years after making the gift.

Generally speaking, the Attorney or Deputy may only make gifts on the person's behalf on 'customary' occasions, such as birthdays and weddings. Even then, the size of the gifts has to be reasonable. Unless the person was in the habit of making regular lavish gifts before they lost capacity, this limited power is unlikely to help with inheritance tax planning.

There is also a 'de minimis' rule, which allows Deputies and Attorneys to make gifts that fall within the annual exemption of £3,000 and up to ten gifts which fall in the small gifts exemption of £250. This represents a total of £5,500 per year. The de minimis rule only applies in the case of someone whose estate is worth more than the nil rate band (currently £325,000) and who has a life expectancy of less than ten years. Again, this is of very limited assistance with effective inheritance tax planning.

Any gift which is significant enough to be useful for inheritance tax planning purposes will almost certainly need to be approved by the Court of Protection.

If an Attorney or Deputy wishes to make a large gift on behalf of someone else, they will need court approval and be able to convincingly explain why they think it is in the person's best interests for the gift to be made. If you were inclined to do nothing while you had capacity the likelihood is that an independent third party will conclude that you would have been unlikely to have done anything before you died. The Official Solicitor or the Office of the Public Guardian may become involved and wish to speak to the person concerned and provide a recommendation to the court.

Having said that, a court does recognise that reducing inheritance tax can be a valid reason for authorising a gift. However, they will need to know a great deal about the person's background and finances and will need to weigh up various factors.

These factors include:

The reason for making the gift;

How much the gift is;

How big the estate is and whether there will be enough left over to last the donor for the rest of their life;

Who the recipient is and whether the gift would result in unfair treatment of different family members;

What the person's Will says and whether making the gift would override their wishes; and

What the person's own wishes and feelings are likely to be in relation to the gift.

This is quite detailed stuff!

This is, you might reflect with hindsight, the sort of stuff which should have been addressed while you had full mental capacity! You would be correct.

Whether or not the court will agree that the gift is in the person's best interests will very much depend on the individual facts. For example, if the person has a long history of being financially astute and, before they lost capacity, took care to arrange their affairs in a tax efficient way then a gift to reduce inheritance tax on death is more likely to be authorised.

An application is less likely to succeed where the person's estate originates from a personal injury payment, for example. In this case, the court's view is that the money was awarded for a specific purpose, e.g. to pay for care, rather than to be passed to beneficiaries on death. A gift application for tax planning purposes is very likely to fail in these circumstances.

Unauthorised Gifts

If a Deputy or Attorney is found to have made gifts when they did not have the authority to make them, they could face serious consequences. There is a very big risk that their appointment will be revoked by the court. They may also be asked to pay back the money personally – in the case of a Deputy, the security bond (a type of insurance policy) could be called in. In the most serious cases, the matter may be considered to be fraud and referred to the police.

Making a Statutory Will

If someone lacks testamentary capacity, then the only way to make a will on their behalf is by applying to the court for a statutory will. This can be used to reduce inheritance tax on death in a number of ways, including:

-   Using the spouse exemption by making gifts to the person's spouse or civil partner or by making a life interest trust in their favour;
-   Preventing the same property being taxed twice by passing it down the generations, for example to grandchildren rather than to children;
-   Using the charity exemption - gifts to charity are free of inheritance tax and if more than 10% of the estate is left to charity then the rate of inheritance tax is reduced to 36%; and
-   Taking advantage of the 'residence nil rate band' which comes into force from April 2017 and which, in the right circumstances, can allow property worth up to £1 million to be left free of tax by 2021.

When considering this type of application, the court will look very carefully at all of the circumstances to decide what is in the person's best interests.

Tax efficiency is not the only factor and may be completely overridden if there are more important considerations.

The court will take into account a wide range of other factors. These include:

- The nature and size of the estate;
- The financial circumstances of the potential beneficiaries;
- The person's likely wishes and feelings; and
- The testator being remembered for 'doing the right thing'.

Again, and unsurprisingly, the court is attempting to address issues which would, again with hindsight, have been better addressed in your younger days.

As well as the involvement of the Official Solicitor in a statutory will application to give their view to the court, anyone who benefits under an existing will or under intestacy will be able to have a say and may well object to the application if it means they will get less.

It is important to remember that mental capacity is decision-specific. Just because someone has an Attorney or Deputy acting on their behalf does not necessarily mean that they lack capacity in relation to all decisions.

If someone has the mental capacity to make a gift then, by law, they are allowed to do this even if someone else has been appointed to look after their finances. Great care should be taken by Attorneys or Deputies making gifts on this basis. They should make a careful record of the steps they took to ascertain mental capacity and the person's wishes. Ideally, they should arrange for an expert to carry out an assessment of capacity specifically in relation to making gifts.

The same applies to making a will – someone with an Attorney or a Deputy may nevertheless still have testamentary capacity and can therefore make their own will without the court becoming involved.

England's Office of the Public Guardian received 141,667 lasting power of attorney applications in the January–March 2016 quarter. It is the highest quarterly figure to date, at 6% higher than the immediately preceding quarter and 18% higher than the same quarter for 2015. In the same period, the number of enduring powers of attorney (EPA) registered fell 14% to 3,511, while the number of deputyships appointed fell 21% to 3,127.

Chapter 5. The Lessons?

They are straightforward.

If you are inclined towards inaction you will probably feel that things will take care of themselves .... and you would be right. All outcomes will now be determined by impersonal forces acting on your estate, whether those forces are inheritance tax legislation, intestacy law or the Court of Protection. All possible outcomes will cease to be determined by you or your family. You and your family will have lost control of the outcome. The tax your estate pays will invariably mirror 'worst case scenario's'.

If you have not made a will consider whether intestacy law ensures that your estate will pass as you wish, whether the people benefitting from this treatment will be content and able to work out the inheritance tax implications. The chances are that it will be a mess. In short if you do not decide how your estate is to pass on your death then you will join that list of famous people in Chapter 2 ... but for all the wrong reasons.

If you do have a will consider whether this is really the way you wish your estate to pass, review it every three years and consider whether the people benefitting from this treatment will be content and work out the inheritance tax implications of your decisions. Generally people will look for their estate to pass on the second death to their children equally. It is often not that straightforward in practice. In particular, where you have been running a business or a property portfolio it may be that only one son or daughter is the natural successor where they have put in a lot of the work on the understanding, sometimes merely verbal, that they will inherit the business. If your will does not reflect that understanding or you have changed it so that it does not, you may well find that your will is challenged and that challenge may even come before your death.

Have a look at the 2016 case of Davies v Davies [2016] EWCA Civ 463 to see what can transpire in these circumstances regarding a botched family farming succession.   This case involved an implied farming partnership with a daughter but the formal partnership agreement was never signed by the parents.   This was followed by a subsequent verbal undertaking by the parents to settle things through their wills. However, the parents wills were drafted to ultimately transfer their partnership interests to a trust with their three daughters as equal beneficiaries. Result? A successful court action by a daughter during the parents lifetimes, no real winners and a split family. As tragic as King Lear? Take a look at Chapter 25 to discover why this case is even more tragic.

You might also consider whether your existing will is sophisticated enough. Take a look at Chapter 23 to get a flavour of how a trust written into your will can secure considerable tax advantages.

Anticipate whether there is anything in your will which could be construed as contentious ... and prepare the ground while you are able to.

Whether you have a will or not, consider whether those who you wish to represent your interests should you lose capacity have any flexibility at all to make or amend your will or to engage in planning for inheritance tax.

There is a common thread here throughout Chapters 1 to 4 – a lack of planning. That will be your legacy .... unless you and your family take some prudent action.

So, there are plenty of reasons to make a will and only one of them is tax. But what you will find, however, is that every one of these reasons carry crucial tax implications and often the consequences are very serious indeed.

The four horsemen of the Book of Revelation are pestilence, war, famine, disease and death. Nice!

The four horsemen of inheritances are perhaps less exotic. They are ignoring inheritance tax (it will not ignore you), failing to make a will, making a poor will which ignores tax efficiency and losing capacity without seeing the other three horsemen approaching.

These four horsemen may not strike the same sense of fear as the originals but their effect on your estate will be just as terrifying if you allow them to approach unchecked.

Part II. Where You Are Going Wrong

"The corollary of H. L. Mencken's view of the complex problem is that sophisticated solutions often obscure simple needs."

Steve Parnham

You have almost certainly given some thought to inheritance tax planning but either it has not yet led to any significant progress or, if it has, you are having second thoughts about it. It is all a bit unsettling.

The next four chapters explore the reasons why you are likely to be stuck … and therefore the thoughts and actions you might consider to take control of your circumstances.

Chapter 6: The Truth About Inheritance Tax

Books on inheritance tax typically incorporate a detailed account of the inheritance tax regime along with a handful of planning points and then it is over to you. The motivation to do anything at all about it lies in how strongly you feel about your estate suffering inheritance tax. Reasonable? Yes. Effective? No.

That is quite a radical statement. I make it because what you have read in these books probably represents around 10% of the picture and it is a 10% which is more likely than not to lead down a road to nowhere .... in practice.

It is also radical because the content in Part III of this book represents an astonishing 90% of the content of what you will often find in books dealing with inheritance tax. It is likely to be a more detailed coverage than in Part III but it remains what it is. The remainder tends to focus on some of the undeniable financial downsides of failing to act.

What you will get in Part III Chapters 10 and 12 might also represent the script or patter of those who have a more general overview of the inheritance tax regime or those who are selling you something, whether that be a specific service or a product.

Part I of this book focussed on the implications of failing to plan, not just in terms of its tax consequences but also in terms of the practical consequences for those left behind. It is not a pretty picture .... but it is one which must be faced up to if you are interested in planning to make this outcome a better one for the family.

Here is the thing though. While that 10% of the picture is certainly crucial, it really does only amount to 10% of what is required to make a success of your planning. You can devote an appropriate amount of time to this or you can devote massive amounts of time to it. The point is that there is at the very least a law of diminishing returns at work here and every reader knows what I mean. You can spend a lifetime endlessly reading the weekend financial press and Googling ideas. You can spend a lifetime talking to ever more advisers and asking them to produce ever more exotic ideas or, more likely, ideas which are merely variations on a theme. This is sometimes referred to in the professions as 'tax as entertainment'. There is always one more rabbit to pull out of a hat to astonish the audience but once the novelty wears off, and it does after a few months of hard slog, there is no magic, just another rabbit and just another hat. This quest rarely involves any serious work on the part of the individual seeking planning solutions and introduces yet another excuse to procrastinate. So onto the next one. It literally becomes an addiction.

My experience suggests that once an individual has a certain level of understanding, adding increasing levels of sophistication is all very well but the payback in terms of decision making and actual planning produces diminishing returns, it tends to flat line. Indeed, the endless search for enlightenment becomes the true focus at the expense of any meaningful action.

The time for sophistication and detail is when you are implementing and executing planning!

The time to sweat the detail is when you are implementing and executing the planning!

If Part I of this book was all about the consequences of failing to plan, on a more subtle, deeper and more fundamental level, it was also about a mindset.   We examined several scenarios and each of these will be different in practice for an individual's circumstances but underneath the bonnet they all have something in common – a particular mindset.   If you have this mindset it is highly likely that your endeavours will either lead nowhere or, if they do lead somewhere, you will just be playing at it. It is a great shame.   The circumstances are as varied as the individuals but everything is driven by the one thing which links them.

There will naturally be excuses, usually genuine issues, for this procrastination – divorced children, young children, young grandchildren, children from other relationships, the unstable marriages of children, I cannot afford to give it away, I cannot trust the recipient. There are also excuses which are more in the mind; the time is not right (consider those well-worn clichés, 'if not now when?' ; 'yesterday you said tomorrow'), no one in the family communicates, inheritance tax is someone else's responsibility, I am only going to do what I am inclined to do.

All are symptoms of a particular mindset.

Even if you are a newbie to planning you will have enough knowledge to start thinking about inheritance tax planning from Part IV of this book. There is nothing intrinsically wrong with deepening this knowledge by reading those types of books which run to 400 – 500 pages and either offer a complete account of the tax in a compendium like format or very specifically focus on a particular area of the tax which may be of interest to you. All I would say is that it will rarely offer you more than 10% of the solution you are seeking. The crucial 90% is within you. So, just be sure that you are seeking knowledge and not entertainment under the illusion that you are doing something other than procrastinating.... making yourself feel better about doing nothing.

So, if 90% of the equation lies in the mindset, what is a mindset?

A straightforward definition of a mindset is that it represents a particular way of thinking; a person's attitude, disposition or a set of opinions about something. It is then an attitude, a predilection or inclination. This in turn governs what you are capable of doing in practice.

It is clear that an individual's state of mind or mindset will be decisive in determining just how successful or otherwise they will be when turning their attention to inheritance tax planning, or anything else for that matter.

If, say, you had a mindset which suggested to you that you would be likely to be 'screwed over' like Prince, for instance, that will determine how you act in your lifetime, even if you spent and inordinate amount of time, effort and money on your estate planning .... which you probably would not.   In Prince's case he did not write a will even though it would have served to minimise the downsides for those dear to him and, indeed, his wider legacy - his beloved music.   He appears to have undertaken no planning. It is not a surprise. From his personal perspective the consequences of his fear and inaction would be unlikely to materialise during his lifetime but it is his family, business and music which will have to pick up the pieces and the downsides are considerable.   It is a mindset which is focussed on the individuals short term perceived interests, inclinations and fears which lead to all the scenarios covered in Part I. At the heart of it is the issue of control. Exercising complete control may be a great, and even essential, mindset from the perspective of someone in their 30's, where you are running a business start-up and leading an embryonic business, but not so good when you are in your 60's or 70's or when it comes to managing that business. It is of no use at all when it comes to inheritance tax planning. In fact, applying the same mindset to other areas often becomes a serious obstacle to making any progress in them.

So what exactly is the mindset which is conducive to inheritance tax planning?

Whatever it is, even if you do not currently have it, it is something which, unlike an effective working knowledge of inheritance tax itself, is extraordinarily easy to acquire. It is far easier to teach than a working knowledge of inheritance tax which may take many years to acquire and is a lifetimes work, a vocation. If you want to that is.

Consider three facts before we go forward.

Firstly, that inheritance tax is one of the most intellectually challenging areas of UK taxation. It has also been said that it takes 12 years to create a tax specialist of any variety. There are then not only, or even mainly, the study and qualifications to consider. There is also the breadth and depth of experience which I will come on to in Chapter 9.

Secondly, that readers who are not tax experts will probably not wish to devote their lives and spare time to being competent in any area of tax, let alone this one. It is a vocation ... or at least it should be...for those who practice it.

Thirdly, that a mindset can be acquired in no more than 30 minutes and is 90% responsible for the outcome of planning in this area. It therefore represents a shortcut, the shortcut, to effective planning.

Just bear in mind that there is all the difference in the world between understanding a mindset on an intellectual level and 'getting it'. Those 'ah ha' moments that this book strives to give you. I can only do my best to convey the mindset to you in the written word. You may 'get it' straight away, it may take some time to reflect on, you may never 'get it'. Also, you may not want to 'get it'. All these are perfectly fine as long as you are honest with yourself…and your family.

What is certain is that if and when you do 'get it' the 10% involving the necessary knowledge will come effortlessly from your own reading and talking to appropriate advisers.

Chapter 7. The Crucial Mindset

I should like to consider four principles which, in my experience, underpin successful inheritance tax planning. Taken in the round they constitute an effective mindset for anyone thinking about inheritance tax planning.

Over 35 years professional experience has taught me that the people who are most successful at limiting their exposure to inheritance tax are those who exhibit to a greater rather than a lesser extent four characteristics working together in tandem. It may be easiest if I make explicit how I came across them myself.

I was never formally taught these principles professionally and I have never seen them set out in books or articles. That is not surprising. Writers on these matters tend to be technically focussed and are almost exclusively concerned with how much tax can be incurred and saved because of the technicalities, but it is much more complex than that. Inheritance tax is often a tax which people will not instinctively see for themselves and so it is a hard sell for advisers and those wishing to mitigate inheritance tax. People are naturally nervous about something which is poorly explained and coloured by both emotion and unspoken assumptions. Whether what people hear really makes sense depends on how comfortable they feel. There is the point. Do professionals empathetically understand where their clients are coming from emotionally? Some undoubtedly do. Many do not.

So, onto the principles.

Principle One: Life is Uncertain.

We all know this is the case really but do we actually 'get it'? It is a hard one to absorb so do not underestimate it.

After working for firms of accountants for 20 years as a tax specialist I had an opportunity to spend some time with a forward thinking law firm. A couple of months before I formally joined up I was asked if I could have an informal telephone conversation with a client of the firm to introduce myself with a view to setting up a meeting once I was installed in my new role.

The client was a very charming businessman in his late 50's who was speaking into his hand held mobile phone on his way home after a business meeting. You could not do that these days. Indeed, you could not have done it then. Nevertheless, we had a very enjoyable half hour chat regarding his circumstances, what he was concerned about and what he was looking for. In a nutshell, his main asset consisted of shares in a property investment company which he estimated had a current value of £3 million. He had become increasingly concerned over the potential inheritance tax liability for the family when he died. I subsequently discovered that the company held over 30 properties of varying values.   He was therefore very focussed indeed on mitigating that liability by diluting his shareholding and the value which remained in his estate during his lifetime. Leaving everything in his will would achieve little in terms of a tax liability of this size.

We concluded our discussion with the businessman requesting that I should call him once I had my feet under the table and had reviewed the company accounts. We would then have an afternoons meeting over some sandwiches to look at the possibilities. His parting words were, "I am fit and healthy so I do not expect to 'snuff it' in the next seven years". A reference to potentially exempt transfers (see Chapter 12) which indicated that he had done some research of his own. A good start.

I never heard his voice again. Two weeks before I joined my new firm he suffered a fatal heart attack.

On paper his premature death left the family with a £1,200,000 inheritance tax liability on the shares alone which may have suggested selling part of the portfolio and distributing the proceeds subject to income tax, to pay the inheritance tax. Tax on tax then. Fortunately, it was possible to buy some time for the family by executing a deed of variation along the lines indicated in Chapter 2. This redirected the shares from the original beneficiary, the elder son and successor, to his widow. Inter spouse transfers including those on death are covered by an exemption and so the charge was postponed until the ultimate death of the widow....but that, and the subsequent planning, is another story.

The principle here is that life can be uncertain and shockingly unpredictable for all of us. I may not finish this sentence today for many reasons which will also hinder, decisively so, my ability to make plans for my eventual or partial demise. While, with hindsight, I have indeed finished that last sentence there will come a day when I will not. One day that will become a fact. It therefore makes sense to take that future fact into account in planning my affairs. It is all very well assuming that you will live indefinitely or even for the more modest next seven years ... but do not bank on it, however young you are. By the same token, none of us can be certain of our mental capacity as became apparent in Chapter 4.

On an intellectual level most people can accept that they are mortal but ..... we often have less time than we think. We understand it but we do not 'get it'. This experience is about 'getting it'. If you have ever been badly injured or have suffered from what may be a life threatening condition you will instinctively know what I am talking about. You get it.

The next two principles were taught to me very early in my career by a kindly client.

I was part of a team which was visiting a landed estate in the West Country. As a junior member of the team I had a fairly mundane job but it was one that I welcomed as it was good experience. It was also an opportunity to get out of a stuffy and confining office on a nice day in spring. As I said, it was a fairly mundane job and the records were excellent and so I was finished within a couple of hours. I took the opportunity to observe my rather unique surroundings.

The halls were awash with oil paintings and antiques but what caught my eye was a small collection of coins which had been framed and were mounted on the wall. I was drawn to them because I knew something about coins and had a general interest in the Anglo-Saxon era. A fascinating period of history and I quickly identified that at least half the collection was late Anglo-Saxon. This made my day and I must have spent about 15 minutes staring at them. But I was not unobserved !

Fortunately, it was not one of the more qualified team members who would undoubtedly have not been sympathetic to my curiosity. Loitering about a client's premises not looking busy would have earned me a reprimand and I had gained the impression that handing out punishment was quite valued by certain misguided colleagues. I was aware of a presence to my right and a very rich voice stamped with authority calmly informed me, "They are Anglo-Saxon, you know." Without looking up I replied, "This one is a silver penny of Edward the Elder but I cannot make out the mint." I turned and saw that I was talking to the owner of all this wealth. We came from very, very different social backgrounds but a single sentence from each of us had established a bond which transcended class. I appreciated what I was looking at and the owner knew that.

The owner, I will call him Sir Nigel (after the character and book by Sir Arthur Conan Doyle), and I talked about coins for a couple of minutes and then the spell was broken. But not quite. The Sir Nigel saw that I was a relative youngster and he wished to communicate something to me that would affect my future in some way. He took me to a room with a magnificent view down a beautiful tree lined avenue which led into the distance. It was really magnificent. Think Blenheim or Windsor Park.

He told me that he could trace his ancestors back to at least the 14th century and some family members said to the Norman conquest. Looking down that avenue I could almost feel the presence of his ancestors. So could he.

"I look like a wealthy aristocrat to your colleagues and in many senses that is correct but they do not understand me. They cannot. I look back through time and forward into the future and realise that I am merely the custodian of the family assets. The family are those who came before, those alive today and those yet to come.   It is my duty and responsibility to preserve those assets."

In that moment I really did understand him. He was caught up in a solemn pact with those who had lived and those who were to come as well as his living family. Get it wrong and he may lose everything his family had achieved over almost 1,000 years. His grandchildren would be told that the family once had stature and wealth but that their grandfather had not managed things well and that those times were a fading memory. That is a tough place to be. I saw the burden for him. I saw his mindset. I saw what he saw with his eyes.

In those moments Sir Nigel successfully conveyed to me two of the cardinal principles of inheritance tax planning. People who need to undertake inheritance tax planning, estate planning, succession planning … whatever you want to call it … and who undertake it effectively have two of his personal characteristics.

Principle 2: Long Term not Short Term

For them inheritance tax planning is a long term matter and understanding that it is long term enables them to put together a strategy which they follow and family members follow. The senior family member(s) ensure that it is enforced with an almost military discipline. There are no exceptions or excuses or indulgences from that duty. One either accepts the party whip on this or you face the consequences of being unfit to inherit and unfit to control. Sir Nigel's family had learnt this over hundreds of years … it is a lesson many with wealth created in the first or second generation have yet to understand. The ability to operate with this long term mindset can confer quite extraordinary power and confidence when managing your estate and the results were and are clear to see.

Principle 3: Family not Individual

They primarily think family not individual when it comes to planning. The question is, 'How does the family preserve those assets?' not 'how do I preserve them?' Not 'what is in it for me?' but 'custodianship' on behalf of the family'. It is the difference between dying properly prepared and leaving the mess of 'no planning and no will'. Personal wealth and controlling that wealth in minute detail comes an extremely poor second to custodianship and passing on a real family legacy.

You may not have to think in terms of 500 or 1,000 years but you can and must think in terms of 10 or 20 years. You may not have to think of many generations of family. Indeed, perhaps future generations should have responsibility for their own planning and take that custodianship as seriously as you do, but you may well think of your living family at some time before, "What's in it for me ?"

Your plans should at least give a nod in the direction that we are all mortal. The businessman I mentioned was in his late 50's when he died. He would undoubtedly plan for living another 10, 20 or 30 years and that would affect his decisions but he may not. The possibility should not only be factored in ... I think that it is actually important in deciding whether to do anything at all.

There is a fourth principle. Unlike the others no one taught it to me but it comes through well over 30 years of professional observation.

Principle 4: The Ability to Appreciate Structured Thinking

If you are going to do anything worthwhile with respect to inheritance tax planning then you need to value structured thinking. You do not necessarily have to sweat it yourself but you do need to value it and, ideally, engage with it.

Structured thinking is the process of putting a framework to complex and ambiguous problems. Why bother?

Without structure, you are like a tourist without a map. You might broadly understand where you want to go (or what you want to solve) in the most vague and general of terms, but you do not know how to get there. You cannot navigate. You are just wandering about aimlessly and become increasingly frustrated. Even worse, the complex and ambiguous reality you are attempting to navigate is constantly in flux. The terrain over which you are attempting to navigate is shifting slowly, and on occasion quickly, as legislation and practice changes.

Having a structure not only helps you to understand the problem at a macro level, it also helps by identifying areas which require deeper understanding. It represents the basis for any worthwhile strategy.

Evidence that structured thinking has taken place invariably takes physical form. It may take the form of reviews, reports, detailed summaries of assets and valuations or the like. Sir Nigel, for instance, had commissioned a master report some 25 years previously which ran to hundreds of pages and included a detailed account of the family strategy underpinned by key legislation and full information on family assets and who (individuals) and what (i.e. trusts, companies, partnerships) had legal and beneficial ownership of those assets. It was continually updated and reviewed with his professional advisers annually. Those annual meetings were never less than a full day in length. Whether Sir Nigel owned these assets or not there was absolutely no doubt as to who had control as the family head. He knew where he had come from and where he was going to.

You may not need to go to the same lengths as Sir Nigel. A well-crafted six pages can evidence structured thinking just as easily as 600 or more.

Structured thinking, then, is the differentiator between effective planning and just going through the motions. Valuing it is the differentiator between someone who takes their planning seriously and the dabbler. Every instance of inaction or poor or failed planning involves an absence of structured thinking and/or a failure to value it. No exceptions!

Yet even with the right state of mind there are still a couple of obstacles which can compromise effective planning. If you know what they are you can do something about them.

These are discussed in Chapters 8 and 9.

Chapter 8 You Cannot Be Serious!!!

Back in 1981, a young John McEnroe, sporting a headband and frizzy hair, was so furious at the Wimbledon umpire Edward James's refusal to rule his serve in that he uttered the now immortal line "you cannot be serious" before subjecting the centre court crowd to a tirade of ill-tempered invective. Brilliant! It ranks as one of the most memorable moments in sporting history. But what can we learn from John McEnroe's cri de cœur in the context of inheritance tax planning?

Doing nothing is often the worst strategy of all when it comes to inheritance tax but it is almost always the easiest to implement and, in the short term at least, is generally pain free. That is why it is the most commonly encountered strategy in practice. It is also a strategy of which HM Revenue & Customs wholeheartedly approve for fairly obvious reasons. It is the source of Jenkins wonderful observation about leaving a legacy to HM Revenue & Customs.

You cannot be serious. ...about inheritance tax planning that is.

I have already mentioned that having some knowledge of the workings of inheritance tax amounts to about 10% of the equation and that mindset is about 90%.

As well as adopting an appropriate mindset one has to take another short journey of three small steps which is simple ... but not necessarily easy for many people. If you cannot make those steps it is difficult to see how you can make progress. These three steps are pretty much intuitive and straightforward where you have the mindset but if you do not they present a tough, uphill struggle.

Step 1

Write down your wishes, concerns and family circumstances on a piece of A4 paper. My experience is that this initial step is best achieved by what might be called a 'focussed brain dump'. Schedule a morning or afternoon in peace and quiet and note everything down on a first draft. What you are looking for at the end of the session is a single double sided A4 sheet with a clear statement on these matters. OK. It might be twice as long in practice but the point is to be concise and clear. Brevity and clarity is the objective.

This sounds straightforward but it is also extremely difficult because you are forcing yourself to write down what may have been little more than tentative musings and the occasional passing thought until now. Giving them physical form is important...and can be a little frightening. If this process takes you more than a couple of hours and/or your final sheet exceeds a single double sided sheet of paper you need to start again ... and relax.

If you find yourself unable to gather your thoughts in this way you might consider whether you are not yet ready to embark on the journey. You need more time to reflect on what is really important to you....and your family. That is OK. But until you are able to do this you will find that it is premature to attempt to push things forward. Those with a short term mindset will never get this far. The exercise is too painful.

Step 2

The second step is to have a fairly precise understanding of the inheritance tax position on your (hypothetical at this stage, of course) demise from the outset. This should flow naturally from your knowledge but ... astonishingly you actually need to do something about it.

Simply note down the detail (the date of acquisition and cost, the cost of any improvements and current market value) of each asset: property, investments and savings, business interests, everything and perform that basic calculation mentioned in Chapter 1. It does not have to be perfect at this early stage but it does need to be your very best guess.

The detail is very much work in progress but you would expect to have clarified the position regarding that detail within three months or so of first putting pen to paper....if you are serious that is. That means proper valuations by the way.

This will enable you to know how much inheritance tax your executors would pay if you died today and how the family would fund the tax. It requires a one page calculation. ... while you are very much alive and in control of the position. Without it you cannot proceed. It can be very liberating to know the score when you have the right mindset.

Step 3

The final step is to have a fairly precise understanding of the current capital gains tax position if you made a gift of property or other assets today, whether to an individual or a trust ... it does not have to be perfect at this early stage but it does need to be your very best guess. The detail, as before, is work in progress but you would expect to have clarified the position within three months or so if you really are serious.

Precise and accurate figures supported by documentation is what is ultimately required, together with precise dates, not abstractions and wishful thinking. Know as exactly as is possible what the liabilities would be as well as anticipating growth. If you cannot write it down you cannot proceed.

In a nutshell, you need to be absolutely clear on the current market value of your chargeable assets today and their cost and dates of acquisition as well as the dates ad cost of any improvements over the years.

....

I have tended to find that where people cannot make a reasonable stab at this from the outset and find appealing excuses not do the work in steps 1, 2 and 3, it is easily the best indicator I know that they are driven by a shorter term mindset. That is fine but you should recognise the fact and reconsider how you are approaching this. The exercise requires some effort and perhaps a bit of what you might call 'archaeology' and those who cannot bring themselves to do it are unconsciously taking a view that the effort is something they would rather avoid. It is easier in the short term, far easier, to play the game of asking advisers for more general discussion along the lines of' tax as entertainment', etc. We are probably all looking at a desire to avoid short term hassle and have an easy life. I understand.

But the reality is that without that information all that is happening is talk, there is no substance. It is prevarication. If you have the right mindset then steps 1, 2 & 3 are simply not a problem. Indeed, if you have the right mindset, no force on earth can stop you nailing this to the ground.

This work is actually, as I have said, quite liberating for many people and with focus could be done in a couple of hours. It is therefore the best indicator I know of not just how serious people actually are but also of their state of mind in approaching their planning. All you will get from acquiring more and more knowledge is, well, a repository of mostly useless knowledge.

To test this all you have to do is ask the question, 'so how much has all this knowledge saved my family in inheritance tax to date?' Exactly how much?

Chapter 9. Your Advisers Mindset

If you are going to do anything worthwhile with respect to inheritance tax planning you will need at some point to find an adviser with a genuine interest in inheritance tax. Ideally someone who lives, eats, drinks and breathes inheritance tax planning rather than someone who has undertaken the odd course on the subject or can spin a good yarn. An enthusiast. Someone who regards their work as a vocation rather than just another job.

Your existing adviser should always be your first, second and third port of call. They know your circumstances better than anyone and are therefore the best placed to help you. All you need to do is convince them that you are serious.

Professional Advisers

What does the world of professional advice look like?

I will try to give you a quick and practical snapshot. That is all it is.

There are very roughly 525,000 qualified professionals you could approach for advice in the UK.

Chartered accountants comprise roughly 63% of that 525,000, solicitors 25%, trust & estate practitioners 4%, chartered tax advisers 4% and IFA's 4%. We are talking ball park figures here.

Not all of these professionals are specialists in inheritance tax, of course, though they will probably all be able to discuss things with you on a general level. Society of Trust & Estate Practitioners (STEP) qualified members are often dual qualified. That is they are also solicitors, accountants or tax advisers. A STEP qualified adviser is usually a good indicator of an inheritance tax specialist ... but it is not the only one and is by no means a must have. Where, however, you are looking for a rough and very crude indicator of likely expertise in inheritance tax planning across the professions then comparing the proportion of professionals with the TEP qualification to the overall number of qualified professionals is not a bad guide. This might lead you to conclude that, perhaps, no more than 5% of professionals will have that expertise.

Your existing adviser is likely to be a solicitor or an accountant.

Law firms tend to be organised by areas of specialisation. For instance, Corporate, Commercial, Employment, Litigation, Family, Development and, of course, Private Client. Look to 'Private Client' for your specialist in a law firm or sometimes the department goes by a more exotic name like 'Wills, Tax and Trusts'. Once you have your specialist the question is whether that specialist has got the necessary depth and breadth of skill and talent for your needs.

It is worth noting that some law firms specialise in preparing wills and dealing with the estate and probate of a deceased testator rather than with inheritance tax planning during the lifetimes of their clients. That may be because it is good, steady business and lifetime planning tends to take a back seat. In such firms it is not uncommon to find that most of the trust side of the business concerns managing the relatively modest trusts which are written into wills and for which an annual tax return is required. There may only be a handful of lifetime trusts in the firms portfolio and where these exist they may have been created by a single person with a flair for lifetime planning who is no longer with the firm.

You can find in such cases that almost all of the internal referral work from the firm's Corporate and Commercial departments to Private Client takes the form of wills for directors and other business owners. Work in connection with the valuable inheritance tax 'business property relief', for instance, may not be identified. Even if it is, advisers may be reluctant to develop the possibilities assuming that this is accountants work since the accountant will prepare the accounts and are responsible for the day to day running of the business.

While this can be the case, it is by no means invariably so. It is your responsibility to come to a view on whether your adviser is comfortable with lifetime planning. Why not ask for a couple of (sanitised, of course) detailed examples of lifetime planning which have been undertaken by your specialist in the last year as a starter? Oh, in writing. It may help your deliberations.

Accountancy firms are also organised by specialism's though the main distinction tends to be between personal (tax compliance and planning, investigations, estates) and business (tax compliance and planning, accounts, audit and industry specialism's such as farming, retail or construction). You are looking for a personal tax specialist with interest in and experience of tax planning in general and inheritance tax planning in particular.

As business advisers no one does it better than accountants but you may need to dig a little deeper for inheritance tax advice. For instance, most accountants will quite rightly regard themselves as business specialists but a business specialist may not be the inheritance tax business property relief specialist … if there is one. Most accountants are not specialists in inheritance tax business property relief but in my experience are always inevitably and quite rightly fiddling with business structures and the interests of participants in response to clients personal, family and business requirements. All these changes will have inheritance tax implications which may not have been fully thought through unless the client makes it an issue or unless there is an inheritance tax specialist within the team. Why not ask for a couple of (sanitised, of course) detailed examples of helping businesses secure inheritance tax 'business property relief' as part of lifetime planning which have been undertaken by your specialist in the last year?   Again, ideally in writing. You need to deliberate on the response and a mumbled 'affirmative' response requires further probing. The answer may be revealing, comforting or, in an ideal world, both.

Asking for Inheritance Tax Advice

As I say above, the chances are that your existing adviser and therefore your first port of call will be either an accountant or a solicitor.

If you have undertaken the three steps in the Chapters 8 your adviser can do little but take you seriously provided you persist. If you have not done that essential work then you must be realistic and cautious over what will happen in a meeting. The reality is that without the information in Chapter 8 even the most gifted adviser will be unable to take things beyond a general discussion, however well it goes .... and that is as far as it does go for most people. I have had the chat – box ticked. Hardly!

Ask that question again. How much inheritance tax has actually been saved through that meeting? Am I any further forward? Invariably, nothing much has changed following a general meeting.

A general discussion is exactly that. There are no specifics, nothing much has been written down, all parties are probably none the wiser.

What to look for in an adviser?

That is simple: Enthusiasm, skill and talent.

Enthusiasm is easy to spot. You know it when you see it because you start to feel it yourself. It is infectious.

So what about skill and talent?

Skill

By skill I mean a depth of technical ability, a firm and confident grasp of relevant inheritance tax legislation and HM Revenue & Customs practice in their area of proficiency.

This is crucial for the execution of specific planning and it is something you may find lacking in a generalist practitioner.

The best place to find some comfort over skill is to look at an advisers offering on their or their firms website. It should somewhere include their qualifications, experience of and interest in the field of capital taxes planning. That represents expertise which should always be taken at face value. There is no need to doubt it.

In this context you should be aware of three potential scenarios where a general discussion along the lines mentioned above is exactly what an adviser may feel most comfortable with, at least on a subconscious level.

The first is where the adviser is a general practitioner or their expertise and skill lies elsewhere. A general discussion may well have ticked the adviser's box insofar as they may feel they have advised you in some indefinable manner. In reality you will know that you are no further forward and that the ball is still perceived as bouncing in your court. If you have undertaken steps 1, 2 & 3 the ball is not in your court. What you really need to establish in these circumstances is whether your adviser is what I would call an 'enabler' or could become one. Are they able to introduce you to another team member or someone from another firm or profession who could work with them to help you? A good enabler should undoubtedly be valued as much as a specialist themselves, perhaps more so.

You might also be wise to distinguish an 'enabler' from a 'referrer. An 'enabler' will have taken things as far as they can before looking around for a specialist. They will often subsequently orchestrate things, attend meetings, etc. because they know their client better than anyone. They will already have a gut feeling for your mindset and will either have some of the information or will play an essential role in obtaining and processing it. Absolutely invaluable for you.

A 'referrer', by contrast, may well pass a potential client to a specialist but will not control the matter or provide much information as part of that process. That introduction may be useful but you are essentially being left with the responsibility for all the other stuff that an 'enabler will address with you as a matter of course.

The second scenario where a general discussion could be useful for an adviser is where that discussion appears to be a prelude to you potentially buying a product or service of some kind. Just be aware that talking about inheritance tax and having a good story to tell is not quite the same thing as advice.   There is nothing intrinsically wrong with products or commoditised services so long as they are appropriate for you and your circumstances.

The third scenario is where the adviser has a relevant but fairly narrow skill set. Once the small part of the jigsaw which they deal with has been addressed the rest of the equation might just take the form of the general discussion above and so you are back to spotting whether someone is an 'enabler' or not.

Talent

Talent is far more difficult to judge than skill but it is just as crucial, if not more so, than skill itself.

By talent I am referring to a breadth of vision, a sensitivity and awareness as to what is possible. Everyone has their comfort zone and a good test of talent is to see whether an adviser is open minded enough to discuss in detail areas in which they may not major in or benefit from.

For instance, solicitors tend to major on trusts and accountants on business property relief. It might therefore be enlightening to discover the extent to which a solicitor is willing to consider, say, insurance based products or business property relief or how familiar an accountant is with trusts. You are not trying to catch anyone out here out but you are simply attempting to ascertain whether a particular adviser is a good fit and has the right depth and breadth for you and your circumstances. You are looking to see if a specialist adviser is really a one or two trick pony (i.e. has a narrow skill set).

There are plenty of solicitors who are experts at business property relief, and plenty of accountants are experts at trusts … but it is your mission when considering planning to judge who you are speaking to. All may tell a good story but you must ask yourself whether that is of any use to you. And remember, it is the particular practitioner you are speaking to, not the firm they represent, which is important in this context.

In reality it may not matter if you are talking to a one or two trick pony who is superbly good at those things if those are the only tricks you require. They are undoubtedly skilful. But if your affairs are complex, involve wealth significantly above the nil rate band or involve investment property or a business then you may be short changed in scoping the alternative and full range of strategies you might employ and in critically appraising which of those strategies will suit your purposes best and, ultimately, in the execution of planning.

You invariably end up with the adviser and breadth and depth of advice you deserve. If you do not have the mindset or cannot take the exercise seriously then you are unconsciously colluding with the limitations of your adviser. And, for the avoidance of doubt, every adviser has limitations. A good adviser, however, will tell you what you need to know whether it is in their interests or not, not what you want to hear.

Your existing adviser should be, as I have already said, your first, second and third port of call. After all, they know more about your circumstances than anyone else and very often you only need to demonstrate to them that you are serious to start the ball rolling.

Terms of Engagement

You might wish to consider whether you will ultimately get a letter of engagement from your adviser specifically for inheritance tax work or whether that advice is covered by their existing retainer.

You need to know which because you may well need to rely on any advice you are given. If the response is anything other than affirmative, clear and unequivocal then you are probably dealing with someone whose expertise really lies elsewhere or they are promoting something rather than offering technical expertise which you can count on.

If you have a letter of engagement then read the terms and conditions which should set out clearly what your advisers responsibilities are to you and, indeed, your responsibilities to them. If an advisers professional indemnity cover does not extend to inheritance tax planning or they do not have the experience or capability to research and execute planning, you will find that the question of a letter of engagement will be probably be sidestepped or fudged. You need that letter otherwise it is difficult to see how an adviser will take responsibility for any tax advice given.

I am aware of some accountants, for instance, who specifically exclude inheritance tax from their general retainer and either do not offer that advice or issue specific retainers in appropriate circumstances. That seems perfectly reasonable to me. That does not mean that they cannot advise you. Only that they would need a separate letter of engagement to do so.

And in Practice?

You should be sensitive to the reality that different types of professional will tend to have unconscious leanings toward particular inheritance tax mitigation strategies simply because their favoured strategies employ a service or product which they provide and for which they are remunerated. There is nothing strange about this, it is their skill set, unless those are the only strategies which are ever properly discussed with clients. They will be extremely skilful in certain areas but, well, how broad are those skills and how talented are they? That is the question and only you will be able to reveal the answer.

For instance, you definitely need a good private client solicitor to prepare your will but consider whether there is an innate preference in the firm in favour of dealing with the estates of deceased persons and probate to the detriment of lifetime inheritance tax planning and tax driven reliefs for businesses.   After all, remember that most solicitors along with most other advisers have fee targets to meet and with every six minutes or so of your time being chargeable in principle,   there   can   be   practical   and   commercial disincentives to professionals engaging with certain kinds of work, especially where these are outside of their comfort zones.

If you are dealing with a skilled and talented specialist you should not have those sorts of concern.

If you are dealing with a genuine enabler then they will be consummate professionals. You will be introduced to people who are specialists and the enabler will be an essential part of all discussions, often orchestrating everything.

It is that simple.

The solicitor dealing with the will based issues in Chapter 23 for instance would, if a skilled and talented specialist, also look at the other side of the equation and prepare a detailed review of the accounts to ascertain whether there were weaknesses in a potential claim for business property relief for instance. If business driven reliefs was something more on the periphery of their expertise they would perhaps have the traits of an 'enabler' and suggest to you that a joint meeting with your accountant was in order to that they could discuss these matters in some detail. Either approach is just what you would want and anticipate.

What you do not want in the context of Chapter 23 is either a simple will with everything going to the survivor or for the input to stop as soon as the will is drawn up on the grounds that business property relief is the preserve of the accountant…which may or may not be the case. It depends on the accountant.

If something appears not to have been addressed then do not assume that it has. Raise the question politely but firmly and persist.

At least one of your advisers needs to be a private client specialist then and at least one of your advisers must have the skill and talent to lead the strategy and pull the loose ends together for you. They may be the same person but they are not necessarily so. If you give that leadership role to a generalist who is not an 'enabler' or someone with a fairly narrow silo mentality and skill set then those limitations will determine the scope and outcome of your planning. You will be getting mid-20th century style advice and service in the 21st century. If that is what you want then it is a reflection of what you truly value and you should be honest with yourself.

As I have said, it is that simple. But simple does not necessarily mean easy.

Part III. The Tax Regime You Are Facing

Pothinus: "Is it possible that Caesar, the conqueror of the world, has time to occupy himself with such a trifle as our taxes?"

Caesar: "My friend, taxes are the chief business of a conqueror of the

world."

George Bernard Shaw 1856 – 1950 , "Caesar and Cleopatra, Act II"

We learnt in Part I that there are plenty of reasons to make a will and only one of them is tax.

What you will find, however, is that every one of these reasons has crucial tax implications and often the consequences are very serious indeed.

Looking back to Chapter 1, what do we need to know about the tax regime which lies behind the figures?

The next seven Chapters can only aspire to cover the bare bones to give you a feel for the regime. Much detail is left out. Many topics are left out. This is not a reference book. The seven Chapters only attempt to provide a navigation aid.

In navigational terms, the question is 'What does the terrain I will attempt to navigate look like?' What is the essential knowledge which can assist with reducing the headline figure which you have calculated in Chapter 1.

Chapter 10. Inheritance Tax Nil Rate Bands

At present, each person benefits from an exemption from inheritance tax on the first £325,000 of their estate, more commonly referred to as the nil rate band. If your estate is valued above that threshold it is taxed at 40%.

Married couples and those in civil partnerships benefit from two concessions.

First, on dying they can pass assets to their partners free of inheritance tax as we have seen in Chapter 2. If Jack dies and his will leaves everything to his wife Jill, the transfer which is deemed to take place on his death is free from inheritance tax on his death. If he leaves 50% of his estate to his wife then 50% is free from inheritance tax because Jill is an exempt beneficiary of his estate. Transfers between spouses or civil partners are exempt from inheritance tax.

Second, since October 2007 a surviving spouse can make use of any unused element of a nil rate band belonging to a deceased spouse or civil partner on their own death, thus enabling a couple to shelter up to £650,000 of their combined estate from inheritance tax. There is a specific form to ensure that the transfer is effective available from HM Revenue & Customs website - Form IHT402.

The amount of the nil rate band has not altered since 2009. Finance Act 2015 extended the freeze of the nil rate band at £325,000 until the end of 2020/21. If the nil rate band had been raised in line with inflation then it has been estimated that it would now be worth just under £400,000.

Prior to October 2007 the position was very different. The first of a couple to die could leave all their assets to their surviving spouse completely free of inheritance tax but when the surviving spouse died the survivor could only use their own nil rate band for the total estate. This meant that when assets were passed to children or other beneficiaries, on the second death, many faced a much increased tax charge, potentially up to £130,000, because of the lack of transferability of the nil rate band.

To avoid this, people often created discretionary trusts under a will on the first death of a couple to utilise amounts up to the nil rate band so that the first spouse's assets were taken out of their estate for inheritance tax purposes on their death. Thus, each spouse's nil rate band allowance was utilised. It was a very tax efficient solution at the time.

Since October 2007 however, married couples and civil partners have been able to transfer their unused nil rate band to their surviving spouse, creating a tax free allowance of up to £650,000 on the second death. Although this change made will based discretionary trusts less attractive to some, many people still use them to ensure assets are left to their intended beneficiaries, such as children from a first marriage, for asset protection purposes or to assist with business property (see Chapter 23) or for residential nil rate band planning (see Chapter 11).

Main Point

If your estate is fully covered by the nil rate band and the transferrable nil rate band in the case of married couples and civil partners, you will not need to pay inheritance tax. If your estate exceeds the nil rate band(s) you will pay tax of 40% on the excess, subject to reliefs and exemptions.

Chapter 11. The Home & the Residential Nil Rate Band

The inheritance tax main residential nil rate band is a complex solution to what was a relatively straightforward problem. For some years, there had been calls to increase the nil rate band threshold from £325,000. Instead of increasing it for everybody the residential nil rate band gives an additional nil rate amount when an individual's main residence is passed to their direct descendants on death.

Residential nil rate bands are transferable between spouses and civil partners, just like nil rate bands, although a claim must be made within two years of the death.

So, for married couples and civil partners, the effective maximum reliefs are:

2017/18: £200,000 (representing an overall £80,000 saving);

2018/19: £250,000 (representing an overall £100,000 saving);

2019/2020: £300,000 (representing an overall £120,000 saving);

2020/21: £350,000 (representing an overall £140,000 saving).

A Residence

The residence nil rate band applies to an interest in a dwelling house that has been the person's residence at a time when the person's estate included that, or any other, interest in it.

Crucially, it should be remembered that the relief applies only on death, not to failed potentially exempt lifetime transfers.

The qualifying residential interest is limited to one property but your personal representatives will be able to nominate which should qualify if there is more than one in the estate. A property that was never a residence of the deceased, such as a buy-to-let will not qualify, of course.

A claim will have to be made on the death of a person's surviving spouse or civil partner to transfer any unused proportion of the additional nil rate band unused by the person on their death in the same way that the existing nil rate band can be transferred.

Larger Estates

There is a limit to this 'generosity'. If the net value of your estate (after deducting any liabilities but before reliefs and exemptions) is above £2 million, the additional nil rate band will be tapered away by £1 for every £2 by which the net value exceeds that amount. The taper threshold at which the additional nil rate band is gradually withdrawn will also rise in line with the consumer price index from 2021/2022. Therefore, many estates will derive no benefit at all from the residential nil rate band and so will need to consider other types of planning. There is an example of how this works in practice and how planning might be used in relation to the taper threshold in Chapter 23.

Directly Inherited

To qualify for this break you will have to be:

Married or in a civil partnership.

Have a family home and

Have direct descendants to pass your wealth to.

If not, you will not qualify for this relief.

That rules out quite a large part of the adult UK population and means that it is somewhat misleading to suggest that everyone will ultimately be able to shelter a million pounds from inheritance tax. Some will. Some will not.

Crucially, to qualify for the family home allowance the property must be "directly inherited" by direct descendants. This includes children, stepchildren, adopted and foster children, and grandchildren and certain spouses. Discretionary trusts will not qualify because the trustees take on legal ownership of the asset in the trust and have discretion around which of the beneficiaries receive which assets, how much each will get and when. The beneficiaries only have the right to be considered by the trustees, who are not legally bound to follow the wishes of the deceased.

Many families who set up "discretionary trusts", perhaps of a type mentioned in the last Chapter, so they could leave property to children in a tax efficient manner may miss out on this valuable inheritance tax allowance unless they make significant changes to their will.

Where, however, any property (and other assets) are deemed to pass directly to the beneficiaries, who are fully entitled to use the property or take any income from it, the existence of the trust is effectively ignored for tax purposes.

The following trusts, where properly drafted, should enable the additional nil rate band to be claimed.

Interest in possession trusts

The most common qualifying trust will be a life interest created by will – this is often seen where the first spouse dies and wants to ensure that the surviving spouse can occupy the property for the duration of their lifetime, before the property passes to children.

Disabled persons trust and interest in possession

Similar to the above, this is where a life interest is created for the benefit of a disabled beneficiary.

Bereaved minor's trust

This trust is created for the benefit of a child under the age of 18 who has already suffered the death of one parent. While the child is under 18, he or she should be able to live in the property or, if it is let, should benefit from any income.

When the child reaches 18 years of age, legal ownership of the property passes to them.

Age 18 to 25 trusts

These operate in a similar way to the trust above.

Observations

You should be aware that the bar on discretionary trusts does not mean that you cannot have a discretionary trust written into your will where it is designed to create a qualifying life interest within two years of your death. That would give your executors flexibility and would allow your home to pass in such a way that the transfer attracts the residential nil rate band.

An interesting last minute planning point. If you find that your estate is sizable enough that you fail to qualify for the residential nil rate band because the value of your estate is too high, you could consider making a significant potentially exempt transfer (not the home) in your lifetime. For inheritance tax purposes the PET will fail because, subject to tapering relief, it was made within seven years of your death. However, as currently drafted, the calculation of the value of your estate for the purposes of the residential nil rate band is based on your free estate. If you had an estate of £3 million and gave away £1 million, say, a year before you died your free estate would be £2 million. This is very much a late in life strategy but may be one worthy of consideration in appropriate circumstances.

Main Point

A relief which is potentially and ultimately worth up to £140,000 in inheritance tax is at stake here and 'do it yourself' wills and the four horsemen will undoubtedly ensure that many will be disappointed when they come to rely on this overly complex relief. Make sure that you are not amongst their number!

Chapter 12. Gifts and Exemptions

Married couples and civil partners can gift each other assets and there will be no inheritance tax charge on the lifetime gift as long as the recipient is domiciled in the UK.

However, transfers to others that are not covered by the reliefs listed below, are treated as potentially chargeable lifetime gifts or transfers (known as PETs). The gifts will be included in the estate of the donor if they were made less than seven years before the date of death and the recipient may be required to pay any inheritance tax directly attributable to the gift. Where this occurs, the PET's which are now chargeable will serve to reduce your available nil rate band.

Otherwise, inheritance tax is paid by the estate.

Tapering Relief

Inheritance tax is payable at 40% subject to a form of taper relief as a percentage of the full rate of tax levied on PETs made between the date of the gift and date of death.

The reduction in the full rate of tax is:

0 to 3 years – 0%

3 to 4 years – 20%

4 to 5 years – 40%

5 to 6 years – 60%

6 to 7 years – 80%

That translates into an effective inheritance tax rate on gifts of:

0 - 3 years – 40%

3 to 4 years – 32%

4 to 5 years – 24%

5 to 6 years – 16%

6 to 7 years – 8%

For example, where you survive a gift by 4 to 5 years you would expect the rate of tax to benefit from a 40% reduction. That translates into 40% (full rate) at 40% (taper relief) = 16% relief so that the actual rate becomes 24% (i.e. 40%-16%).

So the longer you survive the gift the less inheritance tax the family suffers where the gift occurs between three to seven years before your demise.

These rates may be reduced if the deceased qualified for a reduced rate of inheritance tax.

Exemptions

The thing to appreciate about exemptions is that this is what they are. If a gift is covered by an exemption then there will be no inheritance tax to pay even if you died the following day.

It makes sense to utilise exemptions as often as possible.

Annual Exemption

Up to £3,000 of gifts made each year. The £3,000 exemption from the previous year may also be available, if not used in that year.

Wedding Gifts

There is no inheritance tax on a wedding or civil partnership gift worth up to:

£5,000 given to a child

£2,500 given to a grandchild or great-grandchild

£1,000 given to anyone else

The gift must be given on or shortly before the date of the wedding or civil partnership ceremony.

Gifts up to £250

There is no inheritance tax on individual gifts worth up to £250. You can give as many people as you like up to £250 each in any one tax year.

However, you cannot give someone another £250 if you have given them a gift using a different exemption, e.g. the £3,000 annual exemption.

If you give someone more than £250 in a tax year, the whole amount counts - the first £250 is not exempt.

Normal Expenditure Out Of Income

There is no inheritance tax on gifts from the deceased's income (after they paid tax) as long as the deceased had enough money to maintain their normal lifestyle.

The relief is very much underused, mainly because it requires a place in a long term planning strategy and a certain discipline in execution. Have a look at the Chapter on Structured Thinking in Part V to see how this relief can be successfully claimed in more detail.

Dispositions For Maintenance Of Family

There's no inheritance tax on gifts to help with other people's living costs where they are made to, for example:

- an ex-husband, ex-wife or former civil partner
- a relative who is dependent on them because of old age, illness or disability
- a child (including adopted and step-child) under 18 or in full-time education

Again, this is an extremely underestimated exemption and you will tend to see it used to its full and proper potential where the opportunities are identified and planning executed as part of a structured strategy to mitigate tax.

Charities

There is no inheritance tax on gifts to UK charities, museums, universities or community amateur sports clubs.

Political Parties

There is no inheritance tax on gifts to political parties that have either:

- Two members elected to the House of Commons
- One member elected to the House of Commons and received at least 150,000 votes in a general election.

....

Inheritance tax planning is simple then. You make gifts using exemptions where you can and live for seven years.

Or is it?

People can become very attached to their wealth and valuable possessions and often cannot quite face giving any of them up in the name of family tax efficiency. This may indeed be because they really cannot afford to give them up, in which case that is understandable because they may need access to the income or capital which underlie the assets. Alternatively, they may have identified that a capital gain could arise on the gift of an asset ... but it can also be that they simply do not wish to let go.

Main Point

Never underestimate the enduring and short term desire of an individual to own and control assets....at any cost to the family!

If you feel that you must retain ownership of everything then your planning possibilities are accordingly extremely limited. The inheritance tax ultimately paid by your family will be a direct function of that need.

Chapter 13. Problematic PETS: Gifts with Reservation of Benefit

When the government introduced inheritance tax back in 1984 these were happy days. The legislation in Inheritance Tax Act 1984, known as IHTA 1984, is a model of clarity and is undoubtedly a fine example of what legislation should strive to be. There was, however, a huge omission.

Before 17 March 1986, it was possible to make a gift that was effective for inheritance tax purposes even if the donor continued to receive some benefit in the asset given away. This was really a massive flaw in the way IHTA 1984 was drafted and very quickly, in tax terms anyway, Finance Act 1986 was introduced to put a stop to this loophole. It introduced new rules, similar to those that operated for the previous estate duty regime, designed to make sure that such assets would still be treated as part of the donor's estate for inheritance tax purposes.

The new legislation in Finance Act 1986 was designed to prevent taxpayers from 'having their cake and eating it' as it were. Without the gift with reservation rules, an individual could make a potentially exempt gift of an asset, but continue to have the use and enjoyment of that asset; after seven years, the property would be exempt from inheritance tax. The classic circumstances would have been for an individual to give away their home but to continue living in it. By the spring of 1986 that was no longer possible but it did not stop homemade planning based on the assumption that it was a continuing possibility or in ignorance of the legislation.

A gift with reservation is, broadly, a gift of property made by an individual on or after 18 March 1986, whereby either the recipient does not enjoy possession of the gifted property, or the donor continues to enjoy or benefit from it; if there is a reserved benefit within seven years of the donor's death then the gift is caught by the anti-avoidance rules.

So what?

So, the effect is that the gifted property is treated as part of the donor's estate for inheritance tax purposes. This could in principle result in the same gift being taxed twice. However, there are provisions which provide relief in those circumstances.

If the reservation of benefit ends during the donor's lifetime, the gift is generally treated as a potentially exempt transfer or PET at that point, which is subject to inheritance tax on the donor's death within seven years.

The term 'gift' in the context of the legislation can include a sale deliberately made at undervalue.

Never underestimate the power and reach of this anti-avoidance legislation. If you are thinking of giving away an asset but there are really 'strings attached' to the gift, then think very carefully indeed whether you are potentially caught by the anti-avoidance legislation. It will be your executors who will be left with the mess of sorting this out for you.

Inheritance tax planning schemes quickly evolved to circumvent the gift with reservation rules after FA 1986. This resulted in an extension of anti-avoidance provisions in Finance Act 1999, dealing with arrangements involving interests in land and effective for disposals made on or after 9 March 1999. However, much inheritance tax planning continued to revolve around the donor gifting assets but continuing to benefit from them. The government finally introduced as a deterrent to such schemes, in Finance Act 2004, an income tax charge on 'pre-owned assets' (otherwise known as POAT). This income tax charge was introduced in response to certain inheritance tax planning arrangements with effect from the 2005/2006 tax year, although it applies with retroactive effect from 18 March 1986. Broadly speaking, an income tax liability may arise where a person:

a) occupies land or enjoys assets that he or she has disposed of and are not caught by the Gift with reservation of benefit provisions (usually schemes), or

b) has contributed (directly or indirectly) part of the consideration given by another person for the acquisition of the land (often not schemes).

While these new rules were designed to catch tax schemes, they can also catch other arrangements. For example, where someone gifts cash, the recipient subsequently acquires a property and allows the donor to reside there, there will be an income tax issue.

So, if you have escaped the inheritance tax anti-avoidance legislation you should seriously consider whether you are within the pre-owned asset tax legislation. POAT is the rising star of government revenue from taxation as many executors are beginning to find out to their cost when drafting the necessary inheritance tax returns which they are obliged to do.

The forms contain some extremely revealing questions.

Main Point

When considering inheritance tax planning you should always, always ask the question, 'Am I caught by the anti-avoidance legislation?'

Chapter 14. The Core Problem: The interaction of Capital Gains Tax and Inheritance Tax

The implications which flow from the interaction of the capital gains tax and inheritance tax regimes represent the core problem which estate planning needs to grapple with. It underlies much of what transpires in the world of planning.

Capital Gains Tax

Property and shares are chargeable assets for capital gains tax purposes.

If you sell them then a capital gain arises on the difference between their cost and their current market value.

If you gift chargeable assets directly to another family member they will be deemed to be disposed of at their market value for capital gains tax purposes even though no consideration has been received. Their tax treatment will therefore replicate that of a third party sale.

The first £11,300 (£11,100 for 2016/2017) of an individual's net chargeable gains for 2017/2018 are currently exempt (i.e. the gains are covered by your annual exemption). Until recently, the balance was taxed at 18% for gains which fall within your otherwise unused income tax basic rate band and 28% thereafter. Where shares in unquoted trading companies or in business assets are involved the gain could, and I stress could, be taxed at the highly beneficial rate of 10%.

A major theme of the March 2016 Budget was to differentiate between gains triggered on different categories of assets. The pre-existing 10%, 18% and 28% rates remained and a new rate of 20% was introduced but alongside some seismic shifts in who is to be taxed at which rate.

The March 2016 Budget reduced the higher rate of capital gains tax from 28% to 20%, with the basic rate falling from 18% to 10%, in relation to disposals made on or after 6th April 2016. The trust capital gains tax rate mirrored the personal higher rate reduction from 28% to 20%.

It has long been thought that the optimum rate of capital gains tax is around 18%; at that level people are inclined to regard it as more of an inconvenience rather than an obstacle in considering transactions which may be chargeable to capital gains tax. In other words it is considered that at 18% the number of transactions will increase when compared with the position where higher rates of capital gains tax are pertinent. The driver here therefore appears to have been to encourage investment and increase tax yields by making tax less of an issue in the context of decisions to sell investment assets. 10% is undoubtedly as good as it ever gets.

However, amongst the types of property that do not qualify for the reduced capital gains tax rates is residential property. Probably the major asset class people are concerned with when it comes to inheritance tax planning.

If you retain chargeable assets, including property and shares, until you die there is a beneficial capital gains tax effect. Although death represents a deemed disposal, no gain actually arises to your personal representatives. This means that the beneficiaries under your will are deemed to acquire the relevant assets at their then market value or probate value at no tax cost when you die, thus washing out any inherent historical capital gains built up in your lifetime for them. Where beneficiaries inherit assets on your death and those assets have significantly grown in value under your stewardship, that growth in value can consequently be realised by them free of capital gains tax when sold shortly after probate.

Inheritance Tax

At present inheritance tax is payable at a single rate of 40% on death where the value of your assets together with the value of any chargeable gifts made in the seven years prior to death exceeds your nil rate band and available transferable nil rate band. The first £325,000 or £650,000 of an estate is therefore liable to inheritance tax at 0%. This is known as the nil rate band, as we have seen.

Inheritance tax usually, therefore, tends to be a tax which falls on the second death of married couples and civil partners.

Gifts to Individuals

For inheritance tax purposes a gift to an individual represents a 'potentially exempt transfer' or PET. There is no inheritance tax charge when the gift is made and a charge would only arise if you died within seven years of making the gift. In other words, the gift has the potential to become exempt whether the assets are trading or investment assets and whether they quality for inheritance tax business property relief or not.

Subject to personal requirements and capital gains, there is no limit to the value of assets which can be gifted to individuals without inheritance tax provided you survive seven years.

A form of tapering relief is available as mentioned in Chapter 12 where a donor dies at least three years after making the gift. This relief reduces the inheritance tax payable but not the value transferred.

Gifts to Trusts

For inheritance tax purposes a gift to a formal trust, in contrast, represents a chargeable lifetime transfer rather than a PET although tax is only due at the lifetime inheritance tax rate of 20% on the excess over your available nil rate band, currently £325,000. Once seven years have passed another nil rate band becomes available and so for most there is an effective ceiling of £325,000 on tax free gifts by individuals to trusts every seven years.

As a general principle, chargeable transfers should usually be made before PET's so that in the event of premature death annual exemptions are allocated to chargeable transfers rather than set against PET's which would be a waste.

One can start to see already then that there is a contradiction in strategy between the two taxes. For inheritance tax purposes it makes sense to make gifts during one's lifetime. For capital gains tax purposes it makes sense to hold onto assets until you die in order to obtain the tax free uplift. It is a contradiction which often drives people to, well, inaction. Although they can see the benefits of gifting assets in the long term they are not particularly tempted to do so if it means crystallising a significant capital gain today. We will return to and develop this theme in Chapter 19.

Main Point

If you wish to gift assets with inherent capital gains then you have a choice of incurring capital gains tax now to save inheritance tax at a much higher rate or of saving the immediate pain of a capital gains tax hit in the certain knowledge that the price is a 40% tax hit on the family later on and at the (undoubtedly higher) value in the future rather than the more modest value today. Tricky. The alternative is to consider how you might defer the gain, of course.

Chapter 15. Inheritance Tax Efficiency and Investments

It is perfectly possible to retain or invest in certain types of asset where they are treated favourably for inheritance tax purposes.

ISA's

From April 2015 it has been possible to pass an ISA to a spouse or civil partner at death with no income tax or capital gains tax to pay on the underlying investments. Previously, ISA's transferred in this way between spouses did not attract inheritance tax (which remains the case) but the underlying investments became liable to income tax and capital gains tax.

Pensions

People can now also pass on their pension pots to beneficiaries free of inheritance tax in the right circumstances. If they die before 75, not only will there be no inheritance tax to pay, there will be no income tax when the recipient starts to draw funds from the pot. If death occurs at 75 or over, there will still be no inheritance tax to pay, but the recipient will be taxed at their highest marginal rate of tax when drawing income from it.

Certain Shares

Shares in unquoted trading companies will usually qualify for inheritance tax business property relief after two years of ownership. This means that they will not suffer tax on your death. The rationale for the relief is simple. Creating, running and owning a business is risky. Businesses also pay tax and employ people who pay tax and so governments would like them to continue to do so after the death of their owners. The relief is an expression of the need for continuity and an element of reward for the risk.

While this applies to many owner managed trading businesses, it applies equally to investments in appropriate shares. For the purpose of the relief, shares quoted on AIM are regarded as potentially qualifying and so this opens up an opportunity for investors who have no active involvement in a trading business.

AIM represents a big market with over 500 stocks which currently potentially qualify for relief from inheritance tax after they have been held for two years on the grounds that they are deemed to be business assets. There is obviously no definitive list of which stocks qualify for the exemption and so the status of each stock requires regular checking because this can fluctuate. Most such investments tend to be made therefore through a specialist AIM fund manager who will ensure that the conditions for the relief are maintained.

A bit of background.

The AIM index was launched at 1,000 in 1995 and now stands at a little under 750 – a 25% fall over 20 years. The rate of market contraction increased markedly, doubling to an overall loss of 60 companies in the year to 30 June 2016, 25 of them in the last three months alone.

Of these, nine went through financial stress and insolvency while eight were lost to merger and acquisition activity. Ten of them were in the energy and mining sectors.

Altogether, 100 companies delisted in 2016.

Over the same period, only 40 companies joined the market, the lowest number in the last five years, and the money they raised fell by 42%. In total they raised £721.6 million (£1,238.5 million in 2014/15). Three companies accounted for some £112 million of the total – entertainment publisher Time Out Group (£90 million), Comptoir Group, owner of Lebanese and Eastern Mediterranean restaurant chain Comptoir Libanais, (£16 million) and chocolatier Hotel Chocolat Group (£12 million).

Resources companies are continuing to exit the market and the uncertainty caused by Brexit means there is no longer a steady flow of companies joining AIM. Companies have been reluctant to list on AIM with the impact of Brexit uncertain and many have been forced to exit the market after struggling financially.

The exit of such a high proportion of companies in the energy and mining sectors has been a cause for real concern over the health of AIM since traditionally both sectors provided a good number of new entrants to the market.

Investing in AIM undoubtedly represents a riskier investment than investing in the main market and it should only be considered by those who are genuinely comfortable with that risk and who have sufficient funds to ensure that this represents an appropriate portion of their assets. There are beneficial inheritance tax implications and those benefits accrue quickly but it is wise to constantly remind yourself that investing in an AIM portfolio represents an investment with potential inheritance tax benefits attached.

EIS

You may invest up to £1 million a year. EIS schemes are designed to encourage investment in small unquoted companies. You benefit from up front tax relief of 30% and if held for three years there are no capital gains tax to pay when sold. Any dividends are subject to income tax. If the EIS shares are sold at a loss then the loss (minus any income tax relief given) can be set against other capital gains. In addition, capital gains realised elsewhere can be deferred if they are reinvested into an EIS and the tax bill is paid when the EIS investment is sold.

Generally these shares will also attract inheritance tax business property relief where they are held for two years but they also represent a higher risk, partly because they are a single company share and partly because they are start-ups which may have a higher risk of failure. If you doubt this consider why the reliefs are so incredibly generous. There is a reason for them.

Chapter 16. Insurance

Inheritance tax liabilities may be insured against through a whole of life policy. In other words, a life policy would pay out funds to your executors which are intended to settle the inheritance tax liability on your estate.

 In practice the amount of cover needs to be kept under review on a periodic basis, say every five years, in order to ensure that the amount of cover is sufficient to meet the inheritance tax liability which would arise.

It is likely that the premiums required to obtain the life cover on the maximum liability would really be quite significant as you might imagine. Such insurance can of course be used in parallel with other types of planning.

Perhaps more usefully, it is possible to insure against the inheritance tax which would become payable in the event of your death within seven years of making a gift using decreasing term assurance.

You should as a general point ensure that all benefits arising under such insurance and any existing insurance policies do not fall in to your estate where possible so that they are not subject to inheritance tax. That essentially means writing them under a trust.

Part IV. What You Can Do About It

"Ideas are more powerful than guns. We would not let our enemies have guns, why should we let them have ideas."

Joseph Stalin 1878 - 1953

Chapter 17. The Basic Planning Strategy

There is a timeless strategy for mitigating inheritance tax and everything else is really just a variation on that strategy. You can give assets away, survive for seven years, and their value at the date of gift plus any growth is outside of your estate.

It is, however, important to be crystal clear on exactly what you are giving away since this can impact on what is left in your estate. Obvious? Not really.

The insurance based products we will look at later, for instance, entail giving away future growth or an asset subject to a right to retain access to regular payments and this can affect the valuation of what is given and what is retained for inheritance tax purposes. You can also give away a freehold subject to a lease or give away a lease rather than a freehold to similar effect. How these are structured in each case will decisively affect the value of what is gifted and what is retained and will therefore affect the way in which capital taxes impact on the planning. There are opportunities here, and traps.

Chapter 18. Using Gifts and Exemptions

The main way to reduce the size of your estate, and your first port of call, is to make potentially exempt transfers. Gifts of any size can be made to an individual free of inheritance tax provided you survive seven years after it is made.

The key thing is that the gift must be a genuine one. It is no use saying that you have given, say, a property away if it still remains your home. Remember the gift with reservation and POAT legislation in Chapter 13.

Where an individual dies within seven years of making a gift then it is added to their estate and there may be tax at 40% to pay. However, as we have seen, the rate of tax is reduced for gifts made between three and seven years before death.

The practical problem with PET'S is that they work far better for the wealthier than for those of more modest means. If you have £10 million you are more likely to have spare money or wealth to pass on to the next generation while you are alive. For many working class and middle class people the biggest asset is their home and/or investment property and the dilemma they face is that they cannot afford to give it away to avoid inheritance tax without continuing to enjoy the benefit of living in it or enjoying its income generating capacity.

A gifting strategy can be very effectively run in tandem with the use of reliefs and exemptions. There are several one off gifts covered by exemptions which anyone can make and these are set out in Chapter 12.

Grandparents, for instance, can make gifts into Junior ISA's and children's pensions. These work well for grandparents who can make gifts of £3,000 a year with the money leaving their estate immediately for inheritance tax purposes rather than effectively remaining in their estate for seven years. They may also think of making gifts from surplus income as part of their inheritance tax planning, to pay for school fees for example (see Chapter 27 for what is required in this context).

Bare trusts remain popular and effective vehicles for grandparents to pass wealth down the generations. Interest earned from the investment can be set against the child's personal allowance so in many cases there will be no tax to pay. The child gains access to the money at 18 while the grandparents have reduced their estate by making the gifts. For the avoidance of doubt it is always good practice to have formal documentation prepared.

Formal trusts are the next step up and the wealthier individual like Sir Nigel will tend to use a nil rate band trust every seven years, particularly where the assets transferred have a potential capital gains tax liability on transfer. Where there are two individuals who are potential donors as a married couple or civil partners, then there are two nil rate bands available to cover gifts.

However, four issues often raise their heads once one begins to seriously consider a gifting strategy.

1. The pain of losing control over the asset(s) gifted

2. The pain of capital gains tax on gifted assets.

3. The pain of losing the income which the gifted assets generate.

4. It has all been left too late.

We have already touched on all these issues. Indeed, they have been ever present throughout this book. Now is the time to look them in the eyes and decide if you can grapple with them.

Chapter 19. Dealing With Loss of Control and Capital Gains

It is clear from the preceding Chapter that the nature of the recipient of a gift, that is whether they are an individual or a trust, will have a crucial impact on the immediate inheritance tax and capital gains tax implications for you, the donor.

As you should already appreciate, there is an inherent contradiction with respect to the capital gains tax and inheritance tax aspects of the equation. In many ways the perfect capital gains tax strategy for you is to hold onto your assets until you die so that the family can obtain these at their then market value for capital gains tax purposes under your will. Any future sales will take their then cost for capital gains tax purposes as the market value at the date of your death. This is not, of course, an efficient strategy from an inheritance tax perspective as the full market value of the assets will potentially be taxed at 40% on the second death of a couple, subject to your available nil rate band(s).

If you gift your assets to an individual then after seven years the value plus any growth is outside of your estate. Even if you do not survive the gift by seven years this still remains a good strategy for rapidly appreciating assets for this very reason. This strategy has considerable merit where the assets to be gifted are not chargeable ones for capital gains tax purposes, such as cash, and where the income generated from the assets is not required so long as one is happy for another individual to own the assets outright.

However, there are three downsides where chargeable assets (i.e. where they are chargeable to capital gains tax) are involved.

Firstly, where these stand at significant gains in relation to cost, capital gains tax will be payable on the gift.

Secondly, there will be no uplift in value on your death since you no longer have beneficial ownership of the gifted asset.

Thirdly, there is no protection for the assets against profligate or inexperienced beneficiaries. Nor is there protection against claims in matrimonial or bankruptcy proceedings against the recipient of the gift.

There is little you can do about the second downside. It is one of those aspects of life which you have to accept for what it is. You may, nevertheless, reflect on whether this is really an issue if you intend that the asset remains in the family indefinitely. The capital gains tax base cost would, in this case, be an irrelevancy. Downsides 1 and 3 can be comprehensively addressed through the use of a formal trust.

As relevant property trusts are effectively treated as separate persons for inheritance tax purposes, they provide an opportunity to shelter assets within a vehicle which exists outside of an individual's estate.

The Formal Trust

The advantages of a trust over gifts to individuals when gifting chargeable assets are:

Firstly, the trustees, which almost always include the settlor as the lead trustee, are in a decisive position to control the assets within the trust subject to the wording of the trust deed. The potential for asset protection is consequently unsurpassed.

Secondly, the capital gains tax complication of gains crystallising where chargeable assets are transferred is definitely where a formal trust comes into its own where pertinent to your circumstances. A form to assist with the capital gains tax free transfer, HS295, may be found on HM Revenue & Customs website.

The capital gains tax on such gifts can be deferred on the grounds that they are potentially subject to a lifetime inheritance tax charge and that without the ability to defer the capital gains tax there could be a double charge to tax. That remains the case even though no inheritance tax may actually be payable in practice because the gift is within the donors nil rate band of £325,000. This is why most trusts are rarely set up with more than £325,000 worth of assets.

In practice HM Revenue & Customs hypothetically obtains its tax when (if) the beneficiary of the gift comes to dispose of the shares or property because the beneficiary inherits the capital gains tax base cost of the donor which is likely to be low where assets have been held for many years.

It is important to appreciate the inheritance tax and capital gains tax implications of transferring assets into trust.

Inheritance Tax

A transfer of assets to a relevant property trust is potentially subject to an immediate lifetime charge to inheritance tax and accordingly you would be unlikely on these grounds to settle more than £325,000 of assets each into such a trust every seven years because of the likelihood of a lifetime charge arising.

Any amount up to that value will be covered by your unused inheritance tax nil rate band.

If you established such a trust, up to £325,000 could be removed from your estate after seven years, representing a maximum inheritance tax saving of £130,000. You could continue to do the same every seven years if that were practical. Those with large estates, like Sir Nigel, and who are focussed on planning will regularly tend to set up a trust every seven years.

To be effective for inheritance tax purposes, you and your minor children cannot benefit from the trust in any way. There is nevertheless a real advantage to you insofar as the fund could, say, meet the expenses of your adult children or grandchildren that you might otherwise meet out of your personal income.

You would remain in control of the trust assets indefinitely by being the first named trustee. The trustees have maximum flexibility, since the settlor designates the class of beneficiaries amongst whom the trustees have absolute discretion as to how they deal with both the income and capital.

Capital Gains Tax

For capital gains tax purposes, any gain arising on the transfer of chargeable assets into trust can be held over or deferred. You would not need to pay any capital gains tax now or in the future on creating the trust. A huge advantage given the inherent gains in your interest in the property !

Why do it ?

Quite simply for the potential inheritance tax saving for the family with no capital gains tax downside on transferring assets into trust and no loss of control.

Subject to any other transfers that you have recently made you may transfer assets equal in value to the nil rate band, currently £325,000, into relevant property trusts every seven years free from inheritance tax. If one assumes that your current and previous year's annual exemption of £3,000 remains unused, the initial contribution into the trust could be increased to £331,000.

One also should factor into the equation any anticipated growth in value of trust assets over the period in calculating any tax savings. That growth will be outside of your estate from day one.

Once the assets are within the trust there is, not unsurprisingly, a separate income tax, capital gains tax and inheritance tax regime for the property.

Where there are inherent capital gains attaching to the chargeable assets you wish to transfer, a relevant property trust starts to become a must because the capital gains can be ignored. The only real downsides are that there is a relatively low ceiling on the value which can be transferred into the trust every seven years without triggering a lifetime inheritance tax charge and the lack of a tax free uplift for capital gains tax on death.

I have yet to see anyone voluntarily incur a lifetime inheritance tax charge at 20% by transferring in excess of £325,000 into trust every seven years, although it is not unheard of.

Chapter 20. Dealing with Loss of Income

If you are a fan of structured thinking, the obvious point is do not give assets or income streams away if you cannot afford to do so. If you have a cash lump sum there is no unwritten law in inheritance tax planning to say that the only choice before you is to gift it all or to gift nothing. A fan of structured thinking will be able to work out what could potentially be gifted and what could not.

However, for those who prefer their structured thought to be wrapped up in a product so that they do not have to think too much at all, you should be aware that there is a strong portfolio of insurance based products for more sophisticated insurance based planning than we saw in Chapter 16. Although at the last count, there were at least 100 separate schemes grouped into probably five or six main variants, in essence these allow you to mitigate your exposure to inheritance tax while providing you with financial comfort through an "income stream". Investment into such schemes can give rise to an immediate and substantial reduction in an estates value.

These sorts of insurance based products can prove attractive for people who wish to undertake inheritance tax planning but cannot really afford to lose the income streams which flow from them if they were to transfer wealth out of their estates. These options will tend to have appeal where individuals are more around the cusp of having to pay inheritance tax but you will need a cash lump sum to purchase the single premium bond. They allow individuals to retain some access to either some of the capital or a flow of capital payments that can be used by them in the place of income.

To give a flavour of what is on offer here it is worth briefly looking at a couple of the most popular possibilities.

The Discounted Gift Trust

In this arrangement an individual purchases a single premium insurance bond which is held subject to a trust that gives them a right to regular cash payments for life with the balance of the trust fund being held for the benefit of trust beneficiaries.

Because the underlying investment is a single premium insurance bond, typically the settlor's regular annual cash entitlement will usually equal 5% of the single premium in order to utilise the 5% tax-deferred partial surrender applicable to such arrangements.

Establishing the trust will entail a 'discounted gift'. What on earth does that mean? Essentially, the gift for inheritance tax purposes will be based on the difference between the investment into the single premium insurance bond and the present value of the settlor's retained right to the cash payments (which is dependent on the age, health and gender of the settlor and the size and regularity of the payments involved).

The settlor's retained right will have no value immediately before his or her death and so there will be nothing to include in respect of this in his or her taxable estate.

The discounted gift trust is really only appropriate for people who require regular cash payments from their investment – not somebody who might need flexible access to the capital invested into the trust. The investor will need to be aged well under 90 and in good health otherwise no discount at all will be available. Furthermore, the investor needs to actually spend the cash payments received. It is no good keeping and possibly investing these as otherwise the inheritance tax advantages are then lost.

To the extent that investment growth accrues and the trustees take (usually) 5% annual withdrawals to fund the settlor's income entitlement, the potential chargeable event gain on the bond will be increasing as will the potential income tax liability on encashment.

You will find examples of how this might work for you on the websites of most major insurers.

A potentially practical solution where you have a significant cash sum since the gifted element, suitably discounted, is out of the individuals estate after seven years while the retained right to receive capital payments is worth nothing for inheritance tax purposes on the individuals death.

The Loan Trust

A loan trust involves the individual establishing a discretionary trust to which he or she grants an interest free loan repayable on demand. The trustees invest the loan in a single premium bond and from time to time can make partial encashments from the bond within their 5% tax-deferred annual allowances to repay the settlor's loan.

The individual's ongoing rights under the trust are solely to repayment of the loan. Any investment growth on the bond therefore accrues outside of his or her taxable estate such that the strategy represents a form of asset freezing.

In order to achieve an effective estate planning solution, the loan trust relies on the investor living for a reasonable period of time; so that any investment growth accrues outside his or her taxable estate and loan repayments can be made by the trustees to the settlor. As with the discounted gift scheme, the loan repayments should actually be spent by the individual. If sums received by way of loan repayment are merely invested in the individual's name, that sum and any investment growth will remain in his estate and there will be no beneficial inheritance tax effect. If the individual dies quite soon after establishing the arrangement, the loan will need to be repaid and the bond encashed.

Again, you will find examples of how this might work for you on the websites of major insurers.

………

As both of the above represent products, pre-packaged planning if you like, and as they are also investments, you need to render as transparent as possible the charges the provider will levy on the investment and the extent to which, if any, an element is passed on to the adviser recommending the product. As one provider of single premium bonds says, "this can be a complex area" … but it is one which needs to be as absolutely transparent and clear to the investor as the amount of tax which is in point. Good luck.

Chapter 21. AIM and Retain

In terms of effectiveness, an AIM portfolio can appear to be almost a no brainer because the whole of the value is outside of an inheritance tax charge after two years as a result of the operation of business property relief...and you do not have to give anything away. We have seen, however, that there are risks involved.

An AIM portfolio arguably comes into its own where your life is impaired, in other words where you may not survive the seven years necessary to make a PET effective and you do not particularly rely on income from the investment.

Generally, AIM portfolios are not big payers of dividends and the portfolio remains intact throughout the investors life. They are for a particular kind of investor.

If you have shied away from stock market investments because you find volatility and uncertainty difficult to manage then there must be a question mark over whether a rather higher risk AIM portfolio is what you will be comfortable with.

Many years ago a client had decided to take on an AIM portfolio and we were discussing risk. 'Steve, let me tell you about my attitude to risk. My doctors give me no more than four years to live.'

Everything has its place!

Chapter 22. Some Observations on Wills and Investments

Planning for inheritance tax using wills is essential, though it comprises no more than 10% of the what can be done, even when you have factored in the sort of planning one can see in Chapter 23.

With smaller estates that fairly narrowly defined 10% may be all that is required, of course, but as the value of an estate increases so the significance of planning using wills in the overall scheme of things declines. At this level a will with no lifetime planning is a great and essential start but that is all it is.

Planning using investments which have beneficial inheritance tax implications probably represents no more than 5% of what can be done.

At a recent conference for solicitors on inheritance tax, insurance based inheritance tax products got a mention as one of the top 20 inheritance tax planning tips. That sounds fair. However, in terms of the material presented at the conference that tip nevertheless represented less than 0.5% of the detailed coverage. That is probably unfair with respect to the overall significance of these arrangements though the 5% is probably pretty accurate.

As they are only going to be relevant to people with significant cash who either cannot afford to gift or cannot contemplate giving it away outright, they will tend to be taken up by taxpayers with more modest estates which are exposed to inheritance tax and/or those who shy away from structured thought. They are of little use to those with significant non-cash assets, property or businesses. It is worth considering that Sir Nigel did not use insurance based products to mitigate inheritance tax. He did not need to....for many reasons but the main one lay in the way he thought.

If you have a large and liquid estate then you can afford to make more lavish gifts. End of story. There is no suggestion that you are compromising your personal needs by doing so. If your estate is more modest then you probably cannot afford that generosity.

Single premium bond solutions can be great if you want a packaged inheritance tax solution that gives you access to a stream of income or capital and the sums involved are not particularly large (in inheritance tax terms).

You should also bear in mind, however, that there are almost always alternative strategies to those involving products. Where you are being given patter which replicates the content in chapters 10 and 12 and runs along the lines of, 'a long term inheritance tax strategy is to give away your assets but, oops, you cannot afford to do that so you should buy this' does not necessarily follow. There is a huge jump in logic here.

For instance, if you feel that you cannot afford to make outright gifts, you might consider creating a straightforward relevant property trust for your grandchildren. You could make an interest free loan to the trust. The trust could invest in a UK authorised investment funds or investment trusts with low initial and annual charges. What you are doing here is giving away the growth in the portfolio's value so that, over time, as the loan is repaid to you and the money spent, your estate will reduce. In essence, this is exactly the same idea as the loan trust but without the opacity of the single premium bond....and the opacity of the charges and commission which come with it.

AIM portfolios are particularly useful where one is looking at an impaired life or a particularly aged individual because of the advantages of attracting business property relief after only two years. Otherwise, if time is on your side and/or the sums are significant there may be better options.

For instance, if you are looking at sums that equate to a single nil rate band and you like property investment you could gift cash to a particular type of relevant property trust which places the capital outside of your estate after seven years and yet allows you to retain access to the stream of rental income. The planning opportunity emerges from the changes made back in FA 2006, so there is a well-established pedigree, and it is very underutilised particularly for those who have an innate preference for property over shares and bonds. This type of property planning is a fantastic test of both the skill and talent which an adviser actually has since it will render more transparent the depth of their technical skill and the breadth talent to see and run with the possibility.

A good test of structured thinking? You bet it is!

Specialists and enablers with wide and deep skills and talent will be able to advise you. Specialists with narrow and deep skills, a silo mentality, and generalists may struggle with the idea.

Chapter 23. Your Business

The good news here is that shares in your own trading company can secure 100% relief from inheritance tax on your death. There are comparable reliefs for partnerships and other family businesses. Investment companies are different even if the investments amount to a business as noted in Chapter 24.

The bad news is twofold.

Firstly, most business owners have a fairly simple will leaving everything to their spouse or to the children if their spouse pre-deceases them. We examined some of the consequences of poorly drafted wills in Chapter 3 but these consequences can be particularly harsh when it comes to inheritance tax business property relief … the planning opportunities which can be secured through a thoughtfully drafted will are simply never engaged with.

Unquoted company shares benefit in principle from inheritance tax business property relief which can reduce their value for inheritance tax purposes to nil. At present if the owner of a trading company leaves all their shares to their spouse or civil partner in their will the benefit of the business property relief is lost. However, the inclusion of a trust in the shareholder's will can maximise the benefit of business property relief and save significant sums of tax.

Example 1: Tony and his Mirror Will

Tony owns a majority shareholding valued at £300,000 in Tony Independent Trading, astonishingly a trading company. He and his wife, Cleo, jointly own a property worth £1.5 million and hold other assets and investments totalling £900,000. Their total estate is therefore £2,700,000. The company is sold after Tony's death. If Tony leaves all his assets to Cleo in his will there is an inheritance tax bill to pay of £820,000 on Cleo's death. That represents just over 30% of their joint estates.

Example 2: Tony and a Discretionary Will Trust: I

If instead, Tony leaves his company shares to a discretionary trust in his will (with Cleo as a potential beneficiary) then the shares and their proceeds of sale are outside of Cleo's estate. Inheritance tax business property relief and spouse relief ensure that there is no inheritance tax on Tony's death. On Cleo's death her assets are reduced by £300,000 (the value of the shares in the trust) and there is a tax saving of £120,000 under current rules when she dies.

Example 3: Tony and the Family Home

As we saw in Chapter 11, the residential nil rate band comes into force gradually from April 2017 and, when fully in force, will exempt up to £350,000 of a couple's assets from inheritance tax if they leave a house, or assets representing a home of which they have disposed, to their close family:

children, grandchildren and their spouses and civil partners. The relief is tapered, however, once an estate exceeds £2 million. A crucial point. Tony's shares even if they benefit from business property relief still count towards the £2 million total after which the residential nil rate band begins to be lost.

So, if Tony leaves all his assets to Cleo, as in the first part of example above, his estate will not qualify for the residential nil rate band as he has not left a home to his children or grandchildren. On Cleo's death she leaves the family home to the couple's two children but crucially does not qualify for the residential nil rate band as her estate is too large causing the residential nil rate band to taper away to nil.

Example 4: Tony and his Discretionary Will Trust: II

If Tony uses a trust in his will, as in example 2 above, then Cleo's estate benefits from the £120,000 inheritance tax saving referred to above and, in addition, as her assets have been reduced to £2.4 million, her estate can claim £150,000 of the residential nil rate band leading to an extra tax saving of £60,000.

If Tony had had the foresight of adding £300,000 of other assets (as well as his shares) to the discretionary trust, Cleo's taxable estate would be reduced to £2.1 million, her estate could then claim a residential nil rate band of £300,000 and the tax saving attributable to the residential nil rate band would be £120,000.

The total tax saving from using the trust would then be a substantial £240,000. Almost a quarter of a million in tax.

It is important to appreciate that Cleo would not be disadvantaged in any way as she would have access to the trust assets at the trustees' discretion, and Tony can ensure that the trustees know that the financial welfare of his wife is a major priority. The trust assets are also potentially protected against care fees, creditors, divorce claims and other third party claimants

Example 5: Tony's Executors

For the really astute, even greater tax savings could be achieved where the company was not sold or wound up following Tony's death. Cleo could then consider buying the shares from the trust and, if she then owned them for two years before her death, her executors could then claim business property relief again on her death leading to a further £120,000 tax saving.

So what is the second bit of bad news? It is a simple and brutal truth. However brilliant the will planning, it is all be completely useless for Tony's company if significant parts of the business property relief have been compromised by Tony during his lifetime because he was not very good at managing his business.

Costly inheritance tax traps, and therefore crucial tax planning opportunities, abound and they can only be spotted where the owner is regularly monitoring his or her business with long term inheritance tax planning as the driver.

Example 6: Tony Trashes His Business Property Relief

When HM Revenue & Customs Inheritance Tax review the last three years accounts of Tony Independent Trading, they find that £250,000 of the £300,000 is represented by cash. This is exciting news to the investigating officer because the lions share is probably what the Inspector considers to be an 'excepted asset'. To the extent that it just represents rolled up undistributed profits it will be exposed to inheritance tax.

Tony's accountant puts up a fierce and heroic fight and manages to convince the Inspector that 25% of the cash represents working capital ...but the other 75% is taxable at 40%. The executors face an unexpected tax bill of £75,000. If only Tony had been a better manager of his business the executor's bill would certainly have been far lower and professional advice on the matter could have built a sustainable case for a much higher proportion of the cash being working capital. That is very difficult to do after the event unless the circumstances are exceptional. What a waste!

Common areas of serious concern should include:

- Where business property is held outside the company in the personal capacity of the owner.
- Where shares are gifted to family members during the owners lifetime.
- Where investment assets, including cash, have been allowed to build up in the company over the years.
- Where groups of companies are involved.

- Where there is a mix of trading and investment activity.

Poor management of the underlying issues can lead to complete loss of business property relief, reduced rates of relief on certain assets or clawback of relief already given.

The really bad news is that HM Revenue & Customs will, given that the relief is so valuable, go through your last three years accounts with a fine tooth comb as they did with Tony in an attempt to disqualify you from the relief, in whole or in part, where there is any chance of them doing so .... and in many cases they will succeed simply because it has all been left to chance. Your executors are stuck with the quality of the preparation you have made ... or did not. They will be up against some of the most enthusiastic, skilled and talented Inspectors in HM Revenue & Customs. No contest.

Common failings are excessive cash or investments on the balance sheet and inappropriate group structures which can dramatically reduce or even wipe out this valuable relief and expose the family to tax of close to 40%. These often arise as the result of a business which is really successful and that is exclusively down to the drive of the owner(s). What is often found is that the same drive is missing when it comes to managing the business as a true custodian and in particular the tax aspects of that management. If the business owner(s) are willing to take an active role in managing their company there is no doubt at all that the impact of poor structuring can be remedied within a couple of years or so. Many business owners are simply not inclined to do so.

Where owners do not value structured thinking they risk their family to exposure to hundreds of thousands or even millions in inheritance tax on their death because they are not inclined to undertake some relatively painless planning ... the problem is particularly acute where there is little active engagement on the part of the owner. Many shy away from that but it is solely their responsibility. Generally large accumulations of cash tend to occur where the owner does not wish to extract it from the company because of the tax consequences of doing so. Recent legislation has only added to the incentive to take this short term position. The result is inevitably unwieldy piles of cash or investments which on the face of it will fail to attract business property relief with catastrophic consequences for the business and family. If the owners are able to face up to the fact that they have created the problem by failing to develop a long term policy for the profits they earned, whether retained in the company or not, then they can take responsibility for a solution.

For those who take these things seriously, there certainly are good, practical solutions which will make all the difference. The main obstacle tends to be failure to take responsibility for the management of the outcomes in their businesses. While one might well admire what they have achieved you would not want to invest in this sort of business. It would be too dangerous. It is often all down to a single person who is not subject to the constraints imposed on larger concerns by their boards.

A company's Articles of Association will frequently contain rules which authorise the executors of a deceased shareholder to register as the share owners until they transfer them to the beneficiaries. Does this describe your company? You might consider whether a better way is to prepare a shareholders agreement which sets out what will happen on a shareholders death. It is, in particular, worth considering pre-emption rights which arrange automatic transfer to named shareholders and purchase rights which allow the company to buy back the shares from the beneficiaries. All too often, executors struggle to find any meaningful direction from a deceased shareholder/director.

....

If you or your family do not really know the position by the time HM Revenue & Customs Inheritance Tax are reviewing your accounts then your legacy has been left all to chance.

It is a fact that all tax reliefs must be earned. That is because there are always stringent conditions which must be met to qualify for them. This relief is a complex one and there are many hurdles to cross and traps to avoid. It is equally the case that very few businesses which do qualify really capitalise on the inheritance tax saving opportunities open to them as a result – with the right planning. For instance, even investments can be sheltered from inheritance tax using this relief. The result of leaving it to chance is often at least tens or hundreds of thousands of pounds in unnecessary tax .... even millions.

HM Revenue & Customs Inheritance Tax are certainly going to review your business accounts and background in these circumstances, there are no exceptions. Are you gambling that your accounts and circumstances will withstand the scrutiny of HM Revenue & Customs best? Get it wrong, and most business owners do not get it right, and the cost is high for your family.

Chapter 24. Your Investment Property

... and what about property ?

Unfortunately, there are no specific inheritance tax reliefs for property held by individuals or for shares held in a property company. One either accepts the inevitable tax charge of up to 40% or one looks to make a start with some smart estate planning. There are no magic bullets here. Time is your ally if you take the medium to long term view and you take the initiative. It is your adversary and often a fatal one if you leave it until the last minute.

Owners of investment property portfolios are often left with the impression that nothing can be done to mitigate the potential inheritance tax charge on their demise but that is simply not the case. If an adviser has properly taken them through the options: and as a minimum this will have entailed a consideration of the interaction of the capital gains tax and inheritance tax regimes, the use of trusts and techniques to increase the value which can be transferred above and beyond the nil rate band every seven years, the use of leases and freehold interests to transfer value, the possibility and practicality of incorporation, the use of a property company to achieve discounts to share values, different share classes and techniques to freeze future growth to name but a few possibilities .... then the solution to the problem is likely to be in the way you are approaching it, not in an absence of strategies which could be considered.

The key to smart planning in this area is often to restructure the way that property is held over time and/or to gradually and gently start to transfer some of your interest in it in such a way that the value transferred suffers neither capital gains tax nor inheritance tax at the time you do it.

By way of a brief example of what may be possible, consider Tim who owns the freehold of a commercial property currently worth £1 million. He is desperately concerned to start some planning for what will be, at current values, a £400,000 inheritance tax liability on his death. He is, however, painfully aware of his medium term need for the rental income stream from the property and the eye watering capital gain which would arise were he to gift the property to his children. He acquired his property for a mere £100,000 many years ago.

Tim decides to grant a long lease with a term of, say, 195 years, but which does not give the lessee possession of the property until some future date. This is a reversionary lease, a lease with a deferred start date.

The maximum period during which the lessee's right to possession may be postponed is 21 years. The terms of the lease are expressed to confer possession on whichever is the first to occur of the 21st anniversary of the lease or Tim's death. The recipient is likely to be an individual or individuals, probably Tim's children, or the trustees of a settlement with the children as beneficiaries. Until the 21st anniversary of the lease Tim continues to receive any rental income from the property by virtue of his retention of the freehold. On the 21st anniversary he would lose the right to receive rent.

The freehold continues to have value in the Tim's hands, but that value will depend upon actuarial calculations, since the reversionary lease would be expressed to come into possession on Tim's death if that occurs before the 21st anniversary. The retained interest in the freehold will be worth significantly less than the original unencumbered freehold, but the extent of value retained would depend on circumstances.

The grant of the lease immediately reduces the value of the freehold and then that reduced value continues to decrease in value each year as the year of the leasehold approaches. How much would you pay for a freehold which was subject to a lease lasting almost 200 years which was about to 'kick in'?   Not a lot. If Tim survives until the 21st anniversary of the lease, the freehold reversion to the lease would at that stage have a fairly negligible value as a consequence.

So what Tim has done has immediately reduced the value of the commercial property in his estate for inheritance tax purposes and then he progressively reduces it on an annual basis as the year of the long lease approaches while in the meantime retaining access to the income stream.

There are, of course, quite a lot of tax implications to factor in to the equation. Tim will need to navigate the gift with reservation and POAT provisions as well as the capital gains tax consequences of the grant of a long lease and the position if there were to be a future sale. He will need a detailed report and a significant amount of structured thought is to be anticipated.   Nevertheless, the colossal amount of tax at stake for Tim's family make this a small price to pay.

Giving it all away is not usually a very practical or comfortable strategy, whatever the tax savings may be. But you do not have to do that to make really huge savings.

In other words, you need to aim to make the whole thing painless and yet retain decisive control over your property while taking steps to reduce the longer term tax exposure of the family.   All that is achievable.

In the right circumstances, it is even possible to give property away and retain access to the rental income.

Part V. Where You May Still be Going Wrong

"Only when the tide goes out do you discover who's been swimming naked."

Warren Buffett

Chapter 25. Control Revisited

It is almost a matter of contemporary folklore that you would not want to give everything away to your children during your lifetime. You do not need to be familiar with Shakespeare's King Lear or Kurasawa's Ran to appreciate the wisdom of caution in this respect.

But there is a paradox.

The opposite is equally the case where you insist on retaining the same level of ownership and control as you did in earlier days and are temperamentally committed to inaction. Part I of this book demonstrates that holding onto everything without discrimination can be equally unattractive.

King Lear and Ran are superficially about the foolishness of giving it all away to the children in your lifetime. That seems quite reckless for the generous gifters and pretty unhelpful for the inexperienced receivers of wealth and power. King Lear gives his kingdom to his three daughters. Hidetora Ichimonji, an elderly and powerful Japanese Lord, gives it all to his three sons.

At a deeper level, the play and the film respectively are about the tragedy of ineffectual leadership. If each had hung on to power until they died then the tragedy would have certainly unfolded after their deaths. They would invite the chaos outlined in Part I of this book. Whatever they do they are tragic characters and their legacy is bequeathed to their unfortunate families.

The main obstacle to inheritance tax planning is undoubtedly the desire to retain undiluted ownership over family wealth today, tomorrow and until the final days of your life.

However, looking at it from the perspective of your children, how would you feel if:

You work in a business, that could be a trading business or it could be a residential or commercial property business, but have little or no equity interest in the underlying assets? How secure is your future? Will the business survive after the often predictable inheritance tax hit?

Your parents own your home. How secure is your tenure after the parents death? Is your home going to be sold to cover the estates predictable inheritance tax hit? If not, why not? If you wish to move in the owners lifetime, are they willing and capable of paying the capital gains tax (since there will be no principle private residence relief in these circumstances)?

What will happen on the death of their parents with respect to the succession and how will the inheritance tax be paid?

What your children need where they personally depend on an asset or a business venture which you currently own is some, and probably a significant, interest in the asset or business during your lifetime and a clear roadmap and knowledge of what will happen on the owners death. That also means a clear will which makes specific gifts of the relevant assets supported by a shareholders / partnership agreement or similar.

It is well worth reflecting on the fact that Ran translates from the Japanese as 'chaos'. It is the same chaos that one sees in King Lear. Chaos, however, is equally likely to originate from inaction and inflexible control and ownership where inheritance tax is involved. It is just that the chaos resulting from that tight and inflexible control occurs after your death and not in your lifetime.

The short term mindset is, almost by definition, one focussed on immediate advantage and gratification … and insecurity. It conflates ownership and control. If you own something then you certainly can control it. But you can also control that something if you do not own it provided it's legal and beneficial ownership is thoughtfully structured. King Lear and Ran are all about the folly of losing control rather than ownership. Losing control in your lifetime and losing control on your death are opposite sides of the same coin.

The key is that where ownership of an asset is relinquished in whole or in part, then thought needs to be devoted to control of what is given and the extent and degree to which control can, and should, be retained. Control is an infinitely more subtle concept than ownership. Most inheritance tax disasters can be traced back to intransigence and inflexibility on ownership. If your starting point is that you want nothing to change and first and foremost you want to retain 100% ownership of everything then you have created an impasse. If you have done your calculations then you and the family knows, precisely, what the tax consequences of that inclination on your part will inevitably be. It has a price. A big one.

The Problem

Those who are interested solely in inheritance tax mitigation invariably focus on just that but it is often quite difficult for them or their adviser(s) to generate enthusiasm when all they are looking at is a bunch of assets, albeit very valuable ones, including cash, chattels and shares.   Does it really matter whether a family member gets X amount rather than Y amount with the difference being the tax?   This is why the crucial mindset operates at its greatest level of clarity where one is considering property, including the home, and businesses or where there is considerable wealth...or I daresay where one has a music vault.

You certainly can do it for what amounts to a bunch of assets but psychologically it requires considerably more effort .... and there is always then that underlying default setting to do nothing. It is often, but by no means exclusively, the nature of the assets and how their owner regards those assets which determines how successful they are in achieving their objective.

Succession

The vital difference between extremely successful planning and that which is merely adequate or average lies in the idea of succession, of leaving something which can survive you and benefit your family.   A legacy in other words. That is precisely what Sir Nigel was engaged in on a daily basis. This is far easier to do psychologically where the asset is property or a business and explains why the home is dear to people's hearts in this respect.   For many it is not just their most valuable asset ... it is also bricks and mortar which will survive them... or their business, investment property or their intellectual property. Where the four principles are particularly strong in someone, their focus will invariably be on succession and a custodial role for themselves.

If you combine the four principles as you consider your circumstances, your planning will stand a much, much better chance of success. In fact all successful planning exhibits these principles to a greater or lesser degree. How those characteristics manifest themselves in individuals, which are stronger which are weaker, is always a unique combination. But they will all be there to a greater or lesser extent.

Most ineffective planning is a function of a different mindset – short term, a sense of being immortal and 'what's in it for me'. As I have said, it is not a bad mindset for starting a business and the annual cycle of accounts and tax returns but it is a terrible one for tax planning in general and inheritance tax planning in particular.

Here is the thing though. The crucial mindset is not an 'all or nothing' mindset. Indeed, that is precisely what it is not. What will always emerge is the ambition to transfer value between the generations during one's lifetime because that ensures greater stability and security. It is also far more satisfying than hoarding assets. Someone like Sir Nigel instinctively understands that ownership and control are not the same thing. For inheritance tax purposes you need to divest yourself of a degree of ownership as part of your strategy. That does not mean that you necessarily lose significant control. This is why Sir Nigel has a trust created every seven years and a trust on which he sits as the lead trustee. It is why he owns, perhaps even with a mere minority interest, assets through a company or partnership but in which he retains a high level of control through, perhaps, shareholder or partnership agreements and the company articles. Where he retains decisive ownership of assets, he ensures that ownership will qualify for inheritance tax business or agricultural property relief so that the underlying assets are not subject to inheritance tax. That is why on his death his mighty estate will suffer minimal tax....and why many smaller estates will suffer punitive rates of tax and absolute amounts of inheritance tax sometimes hundreds or even thousands of times greater than that suffered by Sir Nigel. But that result does not come without consistent effort.

Be brutally honest about your mindset. You might discover a preference to hold on to everything until the end no matter what …. and that is fine but you should recognise the fact and the consequences for your ultimate legacy. What is driving you is not, as you may believe, issues about control. They can be resolved. It is an obsession with ownership and ownership alone. Appreciate the difference between ownership and control and you will have learnt what Sir Nigel's family, along with anyone owning land in England understood from the 1300's onwards, 700 years ago. If you die owning significant wealth your family will be taxed on your death and a huge percentage of your estate will go to the taxing authority. The same will happen to your children and their children. In a couple of generations the family will have nothing. By the 1350's very few people owned land on their deaths whether they owned a couple of acres or had estates like Sir Nigel's family. It is not enough to own something, you need to manage it too if you want to pass it down the generations.

Chapter 26. Are You Serious?

It is not uncommon to find that someone has the right mindset and has certainly taken things seriously but then becomes bogged down in clarifying the detail in Steps 2 and 3 of Chapter 8 for a particular crucial asset or assets after the initial burst of enthusiasm and activity.

There can be a number of reasons for this but the most common are where the interest in an asset is unclear and where gifts of all or part of an asset has been made in the past.

Perhaps this is best illustrated by an example.

Let us assume that a significant investment property is owned 100% by George who is interested in inheritance tax planning. As we dig deeper into the history of the asset it transpires that George gave away a 10% interest to a family member 15 years previously.   It is therefore necessary to establish when that gift was made, the terms on which it was made and how the tax consequences were dealt with. This can be where genuine amnesia sets in and enthusiasm wanes but it is nothing which cannot be factored in with persistence. In practice, however, this is where past fudges can begin to emerge and they usually do so in two particular areas.

The first is where there is a lack of clarity over the nature of the interest given away. This should easily be clarified by the narrative of the deed of gift, declaration of trust or similar document hopefully drawn up at the time, of course. It is not always the case.   Sometimes who owns the legal and beneficial interests and in what proportions is vague and there can be issues with the nature of the interests – tenants in common or joint tenants and even whether the property represents partnership interests. A check with the Land Registry can reveal that the Registry records were not updated at the time of the gift or shortly thereafter…which is unhelpful. It suggests a lack of structural thinking at the time. Sometimes both the donor and the donee can struggle to find the documentation and even to obtain it from the professional(s) who drew it up.

The second area tends to be that tax consequences will have arisen in making that gift 15 years ago. Either a capital gain will have arisen and tax paid or it will have been held over or deferred in some instances where that was possible. These consequences need to be crystal clear. They will crucially impact on the tax implications of your current planning. The documentation needs to be available and, hopefully, valuations were commissioned at the time. Again, the donor may even struggle to find a copy of the relevant tax return or even to obtain it from the professionals advising or their predecessors.

If any aspect of this has been an historical fudge then now is the time to nail the fuzziness to the ground. If George made the gift 15 years ago then it will almost certainly have been done with the eyes of either George or his adviser (or, ideally, both) being open. Usually, all this requires is determination and persistence on behalf of the individual with their own records and with those held by the professionals who acted at the time. If there is a lack of determination and persistence then the likelihood is that the inheritance tax planning will stall.

Why?

I suspect that most inheritance tax advisers would be reluctant to progress planning in George's circumstances without having significant comfort in these areas because there is another party to consider here – HM Revenue & Customs. If the reporting was done correctly at the time HM Revenue & Customs will, or should, possess an accurate picture of the transaction based on the above understandings. If HM Revenue & Customs know the position and you do not then I would suggest that is not a good position to be in and that you need to dig deeper. As an added incentive, if the position remains unclear you should consider whether HM Revenue & Customs were properly advised at the time. A disclosure to HM Revenue & Customs may be called for....in which case your inheritance tax planning is on temporary, and possibly permanent, hold. It is your job to unblock the obstruction.

If George's example illustrates your situation to some extent then you need to be firm with your advisers and, if necessary, instruct them to clarify your tax position as a matter of urgency. That is what you are paying them for.

Chapter 27: Structured Thinking Revisited

If you wish to plan for inheritance tax then you do need to value the sort of structured thinking which was introduced in Chapter 7. It is one of the four principles underlying the crucial mindset which is conducive to inheritance tax planning.

That may seem a fairly obvious statement ... but I do not believe that it is. Many people simply do not value structured thinking and it is very easy to see why.

If, for instance, the way in which you make a living does not involve the need for structured thinking then it must be quite difficult to see why you would believe it has any use in other areas. You might, simply because you may believe that those areas may be very different to the one you are experienced in and you would be right. But you might not. Why would you value something which you have never previously seen the need for in your life, particularly where you have been successful, possibly very successful, in your endeavours? Surely, everything needs more or less the same skill set that has made you successful? All you need is different experiences, don't you?

The problem is that if you do not appreciate the value of structured thought then you are much more inclined to listen politely to an adviser but not really do any more than that. It is what many do.

If do not value structured thought you probably will not appreciate the time and effort which has gone into any planning you commission, even if you can see the outcome in some tangible form of, say, a report. You may not appreciate that things are often nuanced and necessarily so. Appreciating those nuances is often the difference between success and failure. Since you do not appreciate that value you may also tend to a view which unconsciously tells you that the price you pay for professional services which require considerably less input from you and which you are used to paying every year, say for an annual tax return or a set of accounts, must be a comparable price to that for planning. You may not wish, or see the need to, pay more than that whatever the complexities and whatever the tax savings.

Who knows? But the consequences of not appreciating structured thought are pretty catastrophic when it comes to inheritance tax planning.

But what is structured thought?

It is easy for someone like me to make a big thing about it but without an example it may look like a fairly intangible idea. So, let us have a look at one of the exemptions mentioned earlier in Chapter 12, the regular gifts out of income, to gain a glimpse of what structured thought looks like.

An Exemption

The value of an exemption is clear. The exemption has immediate effect. The gifts out of regular expenditure exemption is one such exemption. If a gift qualifies, the gift is outside of your estate from day one.

If you do not value structured thought then the outcomes in relation to this exemption are fairly predictable. I have seen these outcomes many, many times. You may read about the exemption and genuinely think 'that is interesting' but the idea is likely to likely come to nothing. A plan based on specifics and a plan spanning several years is going to take an element of structured thinking to address the essential conditions and implementation. It is an exemption little used and little secured because people often do not pay attention to the necessary and practical detail required in setting matters up and do not take the trouble to consider matters in the longer term. In these circumstances it merely remains 'a good idea' but nothing more. I have seen people with an annual income of £1 million, yes £1 million of income a year, and modest expenditure fail to grapple with this exemption even though the exemption is tailor made for them. I have also seen people with very modest income embrace it and effectively eliminate their exposure to inheritance tax over a few years. The difference? Nothing to do with the size of their estates or their income or social class or where they live. There is no correlation at all with these factors. It is everything to do with whether they value structured thinking and have the necessary mindset to plan.

Even worse, some people may decide to do something with the exemption but, because they do not value structured thought and certainly will not pay for it, they simply end up with a series of failed PET's. That may be through poor execution which leaves no 'audit trail' for their executors or poor execution which fails to satisfy the relevant tax legislation, HMRC practice or points that have been clarified over the years in relevant tax cases.

So, onto the exemption proper. It is in principle a very simple exemption. Essentially this exemption, the normal expenditure out of income exemption, allows you to regularly gift part of your unused income and, as an exemption, the value would be immediately out of your estate once you made the gift. If you have successfully satisfied the conditions then you could in principle die the following day and the gift would be out of your estate for inheritance tax purposes. There is no seven year clock running which is a very attractive proposition.

Structured Thinking & Securing the Exemption

Naturally, such a useful exemption comes with qualifying conditions. So would your gift qualify?

Lifetime transfers in this context are exempt from inheritance tax provided they:

- are part of your normal, typical or habitual expenditure.
- are taken out of your income rather than capital.
- leave you with sufficient net income to maintain your usual standard of living.

This is not because I or anyone else says so. It is because that is what the legislation states. It does not matter whether you know that or even believe it. HM Revenue & Customs know that is what the legislation states and it is that which will determine what happens in the real world and nothing else. Consider it like a law of physics. Gravity does not care whether you believe it exists or not. That is immaterial. The law of gravity will demonstrate itself by acting in particular and anticipatable ways, say, if you fall from your ladder. The legislation will behave in the same way.

If you look at this exemption from the perspective of structured thought things may go something like this.

The authority for these qualifying conditions is found in IHTA 1984, Part II, Chapter 1, section 21(1) and so may be much more precisely stated as:

Lifetime transfers are exempt from inheritance tax provided they:

- are part of your normal, typical or habitual expenditure – IHTA 1984 s 21(1)(a).
- are taken out of your income rather than capital – IHTA 1984 s 21(1)(b).
- leave you with sufficient net income to maintain your usual standard of living – IHTA 1984 s 21(1)(c).

If you want to ensure that a particular gift is covered by the exemption then it must comply with s 21(1)(a)(b)(c). If it does not it will not qualify.

The legislation does not specify what these terms mean precisely. Very helpful then! If you look to the Interpretation Act 1978 you will not be enlightened. So how can you be clear and certain on the operating definitions?

Have a look at what HM Revenue & Customs say. HM Revenue & Customs' Inheritance Tax Manual is available online and you might profitably give considerable time to reviewing:

Paragraph 14241 – on what is 'normal'.

Paragraph 14242 – on what represents a 'pattern'.

Paragraph 14243 – on other factors.

Paragraph 14250 – what 'out of income' means.

Paragraph 14255 – what 'standard of living' means

You would also want to be fluent with tax cases which consider the exemption in detail where claims are contested by HM Revenue & Customs such as Bennett v IRC and MacDowell & Others v CIR.

Within that legislative framework and understanding of HM Revenue & Customs practice you will then need to position the gifts you are proposing to make – their anticipated dates and amounts, the recipient. You will also need to prepare a spreadsheet showing annual income, expenditure and the surplus/deficit so that you can comply with s 21(1)(c).

You would be well advised to have a deed of gift or similar document prepared stating that you are making a gift of that amount and at a specific date to a stated beneficiary. It might also be a good idea to have a copy of relevant bank statements appended to your records showing the payment being made and at some point a signed and dated letter to the effect that the gift is being made within the exemption at s 21.

In practice an specialist adviser will be able to do the necessary work for you and ensure compliance with the legislation and HM Revenue & Customs practice but you would also need to do your bit. Hard going? Not at all. Once you have set up your spreadsheet recording your income and expenditure it will not take long to update and monitor your records on an annual basis.

A taxpayer with income of £120,000, for example who can live on £70,000 a year could decide to give away £50,000 each year. In four years he or she would have gifted £200,000 at a tax saving of £80,000 even if he or she died in the fifth tax year. Think of what the individual with an annual income of £1 million could have achieved. That is a lot of money saved. It is well worth a bit of effort. It was also one of Sir Nigel's favourites ... he was not a great hoarder of cash.

Have you done all that? Is it written down and signed off? Do you review and update it annually?

Overkill?

Hardly because there will be two massive obstacles to overcome when you die.

The first is what your executors face.

If you wish to claim this exemption it is certainly strongly advisable to prepare detailed accounts of income and expenditure for each year and to keep receipts. When executors complete Form IHT 400 they will also have to complete a separate Form IHT403. Like all inheritance tax forms, it is well worth having a quick look at it while you are alive. Unless you are fairly meticulous it may be difficult if not impossible for your executors to establish payments and their nature in practice after the event. It is much better to have a disciplined plan which is well documented. Attention to the detail which emerges from structured thought almost serves to instruct the executors to claim the exemption, indeed they may be negligent not to in these circumstances, and gives them the best possible chance of achieving a result quickly and without too much debate with HM Revenue & Customs. You have made it easy for HM Revenue & Customs to see what you have done, how you have complied with their expectations and have pretty much invited them to agree with you that it is effective.

What executors will usually face, however, is an uphill struggle to understand and verify what has occurred in practice and what has been done. If there is little concrete evidence and what there is looks scrappy they will often simply not pursue a weak case. Winding up the estate could take much, much longer and your executors will be under almost daily pressure from other family members to 'get on with it.' If your past actions and records are unable to convince your executors then what chance will they have of convincing HM Revenue & Customs?

The second is what HM Revenue & Customs see. Even if you do not value structured thought, HM Revenue & Customs certainly does and you should assume that they will seek to satisfy themselves that what your executors have put in the IHT403 is verifiable. That is why an ill thought through and scrappy gifting strategy rarely achieves anything. Remember the old military adage, "A poor plan well executed is infinitely preferable to brilliant plan poorly executed." How much easier for everyone if you have a small file of documentation based on the above to back up your executors. It will win hands down, every time.

This is a simple and straightforward exemption and yet whether it is an effective one depends critically on how things are executed. It is little used simply because either no thought has gone into it or, if advice has been taken, the taxpayer decides to implement it themselves without further input from an adviser. What could go wrong? That is a bit like commissioning an architect to draw up a plan for a house and then deciding to make a start without too much building knowledge. I am not sure that I would look forward to residing in it.

The advantages of structured thinking move from being desirable, as in the above instance, to absolutely essential once one moves beyond a straightforward exemption to more complex circumstances. My advice is to value it and even come to love it, not only in yourself but also in your adviser.

Sir Nigel loved the annual meetings which were called to regularly review his estate and the family wealth. He was, of course, a leader when it came to structured thought and respected it in his advisers. However, woe betide any adviser who was less mentally agile or unsure of detail than he. He was and is in a completely different class and a completely different league to King Lear and Hidetora Ichimonji.

Part VI. What Is To Be Done?

"Dare to know! Have the courage to use your own understanding. That is the motto of the Enlightenment."

Immanuel Kant

Students of Russian history will no doubt recognize 'What Is To Be Done?' as the title of one of Lenin's books. Say what you like about the Bolsheviks, they were really adept at snappy titles for their books. There any relevance to inheritance tax ends.

Should you be doing anything then? It all depends on you and your circumstances.

There is a simple test which can be applied to ascertain whether you should be doing anything in principle. I call this the Jenkins test and it is derived from the intriguing quote at the beginning of the book. My experience is that your family will inevitably start to question your handling of your estate from day one following your demise where the inheritance tax hit is somewhere between the lower of £20,000 and 5% of your wealth. At that point it starts to look as though you have actually chosen to make a legacy to the Treasury ... this is, after all, a voluntary levy.

£20,000 is easy to understand. It is the price of a pretty decent car. 5% of your estate is essentially the anticipated inheritance tax divided by the value of your estate and shown as a percentage. It ignores the potential effect of the residential nil rate band.

A single person with a nil rate band of £325,000 and an estate of £375,000 would pay tax of £20,000 or 5% of their estate. A couple passing their estate to the survivor would have two nil rate bands on the second death. If their estate were £750,000 they would pay £40,000 in tax which would also represent 5% of their estate. If their estate were £1 million that percentage would rise to 14%, £1.5 million 23% and £2 million 27%.

The Jenkins test therefore suggests that the crucial figures for the purposes of planning is in the region of an estate of £750,000 for a couple and £375,000 for a single person. A couple for these purposes includes widow or widower entitled to their deceased spouse's or civil partners nil rate band.

So the first thing you should do is apply the Jenkins test to your particular circumstances. That will tell you what the actual position is. Although the Jenkins test is a fairly good measure of when you might be sensible in looking at planning, the reality is that the lower the amount of tax and effective rate of tax, the more likely you will be to shrug and do nothing because at some point you will need to take matters seriously and seek professional advice. It is understandably easier to seek that advice where your exposure to inheritance tax is, say, £50,000 of tax or more than it is if it were a mere £20,000 ... whatever the family thinks on your demise. One therefore tends to find that in practice enthusiasm for doing something starts to arise where a joint estate is around £850,000 or getting on for 10% of an estate. That makes good sense. You are seeking to mitigate inheritance tax, not eliminate it and eliminate it at any cost.

Second, you should ensure that you stand the best chance possible of securing the residential nil rate band for your home whatever the size of your estate. Within a few years this will ultimately relieve up to £350,000 of value with respect to your home and so is worth £140,000 in inheritance tax saved to a couple. By 2020/2021 this suggests that where a couple has a house and children, once a will is in place and planning to get the residential nil rate band is rock solid, worthwhile planning will tend to occur sharply after an estate has reached £1 million or more. As a brief guide, it is likely that by 2020/21 the Jenkins test would anticipate that the impetus to engage in serious inheritance tax planning would become irresistible where joint estates are in the region of £1,050,000 - £1,150,000 or above.

Third, if you have exposure to inheritance tax you might consider a simple, sensible and regular gifting strategy to children and grandchildren, using reliefs and exemptions and subject of course to you being able to afford to do so. There is no point at all in inviting penury for the sake of tax efficiency. Spending it, I have been told, can also be tax efficient, though this approach is not highly prised by those hoping to inherit for some reason.

Fourth, where the Jenkins test indicates a significant issue and larger amounts are involved, where there are capital gains tax implications in gifting assets or investment property or where a business is involved, whether trading or investment in nature, you will need to consider more sophisticated planning and take advice regardless of the Jenkins test.

Fifth, choose your long tern inheritance tax adviser in this area carefully and remember:

Most professionals are not inheritance tax specialists....but they may be brilliant enablers.

Most businesses and investment property holders do not obtain specialist advice. They either believe, or gradually get the feeling from their advisers that, 'there is nothing much which can be done'.

It is your responsibility to select the advisers which are most consistent with your mindset and desired outcome. People actually do this quite naturally in the long run. They have the adviser(s) they deserve. Karma! If you find that your mindset, whatever it is, feels different to that of your adviser then in the longer term you will find that things change....one way or the other. You will change or you will change your adviser.

Finally, work out your potential exposure to tax today. Plan for the next 10-20 years to protect your family from that exposure. During those years attract legitimate tax reliefs and exemptions through sensible and robust planning, think through a practical succession strategy for the family particularly where a business of some sort is involved while staying in control and use your greatest strength, your family, to preserve the very wealth it benefits from, for future generations.

That means working with advisers who can go way beyond the tame stories in chapters 10 and 12 and from whose skill and talent you can benefit from. You know how to choose them and the journey will, or should be, an enjoyable one.

Thank You

Before we part company, I would like to say "thank you" for purchasing my book and reading all the way through it to the end. If you have found this book useful I should be extremely grateful if you would take a minute or two of your time to leave a review on Amazon. It means a lot. Thank you.

No book I have ever read is perfect and this one is no exception. If there are any oversights, omissions or errors or anything you would like to see covered or changed, please email me at stevesbooks@gmail.com.

About the Author

Steve is a practicing UK tax adviser, a writer and blogger.

He believes that words can change the way people see the world, their mindset, and that this can have profound consequences.

Mindset may be defined as a particular way of thinking, a person's attitude or inclination about something. Change this, even slightly, and the world becomes a different place.

Printed in Germany
by Amazon Distribution
GmbH, Leipzig